My Journey to the Black Madonna

A Memoir

Elaine Soto

Copyright © 2020 Elaine Soto
Albuquerque, NM
All rights reserved.
ISBN: 9781791952167

DEDICATION

To the Mighty I Am Presence

To Our Lady of Montserrat

To Jesus and Mary Magdalene

To my Inner Guidance

To my Red Hat Mama

To my loving Husband, Nan

Amor

CONTENTS

	Acknowledgments	i
	Amor	Pg. #3
1	I Saw the Madonna	Pg. #5
2	The Black Madonna	Pg. #14
3	Serendipity	Pg. #18
4	The English Paper	Pg. #24
5	College	Pg. #33
6	Looking for my Father	Pg. #39
7	Puerto Rico	Pg. #48
8	China	Pg. #67
9	Montserrat Spain	Pg. #75
10	Papi Left	Pg. #84
11	Zaragoza Spain	Pg. #94
12	Spain 1999	Pg. #107
13	Italy	Pg. #116
14	France	Pg. #129
15	Mary Magdalene	Pg.#152
16	Healing	Pg. #164

| About the Author | P. #183 |
| Bibliography | P. #184 |

My Journey to the Black Madonna

ACKNOWLEDGMENTS

Ford Foundation Doctoral Fellowship Program

The Center for Puerto Rican Studies

Taller Boricua, Marcos Dimas, Fernando Salicrup, and Irma Ayala

Jorge Soto Sanchez, my brother in Spirit

Sarah Lewis, Photographer

Diogenes Ballester, Artist and Friend

2004 The Mighty Muse Writing Project, Publication Prize "The English Paper".

Elena Avila, Curandera

My Albuquerque Writers Group-Valerie Storey, Sue Blazier, Nance Elsinger, Pat Young, Terry Hicks & Lia Moldovan

Valerie Martinez, Poetess and Teacher

Elaine Soto

"Poetry puts starch in your backbone
so you can stand,
so, you can compose your life."
Maya Angelou

My Journey to the Black Madonna

Amor

>Amor the dark mistress
>Hidden underground
>The source of light and inspiration
>The magnetism …of the universe
>
>Hidden underground
>Life is a journey
>The magnetism …of the universe
>Says we must find our dark secret
>
>Life is a journey
>She is the compassionate one
>Says we must find our dark secret
>The possibility of wisdom
>
>She is the compassionate one
>Darkness is the realm of transformation
>The possibility of wisdom
>Transformation brings
>
>Darkness is the realm of transformation
>The source of light and inspiration
>Transformation brings
>Amor, the dark mistress[1]

---

[1] All the poems in this book are pantoum. A pantoum is a poetic form from 15th Century Malaysia. The poem is of any length composed of four-line stanzas in which the second and fourth line of each stanza serve as the first and third line of the

Elaine Soto

---

next stanza. The last line of the pantoum is the same as the first or third line. It is a circular way of storytelling that evoked unconscious memories and feelings for me.

1 I SAW THE MADONNA

1958

The cab drove down a weeping willow-lined road. We got out and walked up the narrow path to the entrance of Mary Help of Christians Academy. We were carrying suitcases filled with our new uniforms and underwear. This was to be our new home. My mother landed a job working for L'Oréal of Paris in Puerto Rico. This all happened extremely fast.

Mami came home from work smiling and happy. She didn't usually come home like this. Most of the time she came home cranky. Small things like dirty dishes annoyed her. This day in early June, she said. "Girls we need to talk. I got a great job offer from L'Oréal of Paris to work as a hair color technician in Puerto Rico. They will be paying me very well. With this job I can afford to send you to a good school." Education was very important to Mami. She was only able to finish the third grade in Puerto Rico.

Grandpa didn't believe a woman needed an education. He believed that a woman's place was at home caring for her husband and children. "There is a boarding school in Puerto Rico called Academia del Perpetuo Socorro. It is very good. If you go to school there, we will be closer to each other. If we move to Puerto Rico you can attend that school, but you will have to read and write in Spanish. There is also a good boarding school in New Jersey that my friend in Beauty School recommended. She sent her daughter there. There you can study in English like you are doing at St. Luke's, but I will be far away in Puerto Rico. Of course, I will visit you whenever I can."

Peggy and I looked down. I didn't like the thought of separating from Mami. I had already lost my father when I was 3 years old. My parents divorced because my mother didn't accept his infidelity. When we were all together, they spoke Spanish at home. They both migrated from Puerto Rico looking for work. I could read and speak Spanish when I started school. But, after 7 years of studying in English, I wasn't as fluent in Spanish anymore. Peggy and I left the room and spoke in our bedroom. "What do you think, Peggy?"

"I don't know. I am going to leave all my friends if we go to Puerto Rico. " Peggy was pretty like my mother and very popular. I was also pretty, but I had darker hair and an olive complexion, and I was very shy. If you stared at me I could cry.

"I know. If we go to Puerto Rico, we are going to have to learn everything in Spanish and I don't speak Spanish anymore. It was hard enough learning to speak English when I started school here. If we stay here, we can at least study in English."

"I will miss Mami if we stay here," Peggy said.

"Yeah, me too, but Mami has been very sad because she worries about paying the bills. Papi left and he doesn't help her."

"Yeah, I know."

"The other night I had a nightmare. I went to her room and I found her praying and crying. It would be better if she got a good job, so she doesn't worry so much about money." Peggy nodded in agreement. We went back to the living room. Mami was sitting on the green floral couch smoking a Chesterfield cigarette. Her face hidden in a haze of smoke.

"Mami, we want to go to school in New Jersey. There we will be able to speak English and understand the teachers."

Mami looked down and her shoulders drooped. A tear glistened on her cheek. After a while, she said, "Okay then. I will call the school."

At the end of August, we were knocking on the door of the boarding school. Sister Rose, a plump red-cheeked nun greeted us at the door with a warm welcoming smile. Mami filled out the required paperwork and gave her a check for the tuition. She kissed us goodbye, turned around, and walked to the waiting cab. We looked at the rear of the cab as it drove away down the road lined with weeping willows. Mom looked straight ahead as she wiped her cheek with her hand. Sister Rose gave me her handkerchief. She helped us carry our suitcases up the stairs. I blew my nose as we followed on creaking mahogany steps. Sister Rose dressed in the white habit of the Salesian Order. We followed behind the skirt of her floor-length white habit. When we reached the top of the stairs, she smiled at us.

"This is the dormitory," she said. On the landing, there was a beautiful eight-foot-tall painting. It was of an angel accompanying a young boy and girl walking alone in the woods. Sister Rose escorted us into a small room. "I will leave your suitcases here." The room had large wooden cubby holes built into the wall. "This is where Margarita will put your clothes." She said pointing at two empty one-foot square cubby holes labeled with our names. A short, plump woman walked over from a long wooden worktable where she was folding clothes. She wore her gray hair in braids wrapped around her head. She looked at us through silver wire-rimmed glasses.

"Hola muchachas, bienvenidas," she said.

"Margarita, these are Peggy and Elaine. Margarita works in the dormitory and takes care of your clothes and anything you might need. She speaks Spanish.

She accompanied two girls who came from Cuba. Are your clothes labeled with your name?"

"Yes. Mami sewed white labels with our names on all our clothes."

"Very good. There are a lot of girls here and we want to make sure you don't lose your clothes when we do the laundry." She waved her arm directing us to the doorway of a huge rectangular room. "This is the Dormitory." The room had 8-foot-tall wooden windows lining the walls on two sides. The windows on the right showcased huge pine trees and a couple of deer nibbling berries from a nearby bush.

"Look," I said, pointing to the deer. Sr. Rose glanced out the window and smiled.

"The deer like to visit the grounds. They love the gooseberries."

The windows on the left faced a courtyard with a well-maintained lawn. It was the main entrance to the building. In the courtyard, there was a well-pruned lawn and a long concrete path circled around it. Not far from the path, concrete steps led down to a small chapel. The dormitory smelled of fresh linen and Jergens hand lotion. As we walked around the dormitory, we saw row after row of aligned sky-blue metal beds. They had matching nightstands and maple curved back chairs. There were no pictures or objects on the white walls or the nightstands. The room was clean and immaculate.

"We divided the dormitory into sections by grade. These are the beds for the sixth graders. Elaine, this is your bed. Peggy your bed is across the room near the windows with the fourth graders. She left me by my bed and walked Peggy to hers. Peggy and I looked at each other from across the room. She had an expressionless, unsmiling look on her face. I rubbed my elbow scratching an itch I didn't have. I stared at her. At home, we shared a bed. Later, when my father bought the court-mandated bunk beds, Peggy slept on the top bunk and I slept on the bottom one. This was the first time we wouldn't be sleeping together. That night I lay awake, unable to sleep. I was listening to the various snores of the girls that I didn't know. I heard footsteps near my bed. Then a familiar voice whispered.

"Can I sleep with you?" It was Peggy. I could see in the night light tears were running down her cheeks. I moved over in the single bed making room for her. She snuggled up close to me and we covered ourselves with the sheet and blue coverlet.

"I miss Mami."

"Me too," I whispered. We were 16 months apart in age, but it was my job to take care of her while Mami worked. We fell asleep. At 5 am Sister Josephine rang the hand bell. Next, I heard the flipping of light switches and all the lights in the room went on like on a stage. It was time to get up. We made our beds and dressed for morning Mass. Mass was every morning at 6 am in the chapel. As I was making my bed, Sr. Fernanda gestured with her finger for me to come over to her. Her skin was translucent white and she wore wire-rimmed glasses on her long thin nose. She was a serious but handsome nun.

"I saw you and your sister were sleeping together this morning. You can't let her sleep with you."

"She was crying," I said. I didn't tell her that I was crying too.

"I know it is hard, but she has to adjust." Her eyes were soft and kind, but she meant what she said.

After mass, I spoke with Peggy.

"Sister Fernanda says we can't sleep together. She said you have to learn to sleep alone."

"But we always sleep together!"

"I know, but we can't sleep together anymore."

"Okay," she said in an emotion-choked voice. Tears filled my eyes as I watched her walk away. We didn't sleep together again. I missed her and Mom a lot, but at least I saw my sister. I tossed and turned every night. I couldn't sleep. Carmen, a pretty girl with tan skin and long black hair walked over to me one morning. She handed me a prayer card. It had the picture of a beautiful Madonna wearing a turquoise blue cloak. She held a baby in swaddling clothes in her arms.

"I want you to have this. She is famous for miracles. I pray to her and she helps me," she said.

"Thank you, Carmen." I tucked the card of the turquoise-robed Madonna under my pillow. That night as I tossed and turned in the bed, I felt the card under my pillow and pulled it out. I prayed to her every night as tears flowed down my cheeks. One night as I was praying and crying, I saw a dazzling white light near the dormitory windows. I thought it was Sister Fernanda making the rounds with a flashlight, but it wasn't her. I kept looking in the direction of the light and the light became brighter and brighter. The shape of a woman emerged. It was a beautiful woman with a turquoise cloak over her head and shoulders. She held a baby swaddled in a blanket. It was the Madonna from the prayer card, The Madonna of the Streets. At first, I couldn't believe my eyes and I stared at her. She stared at me with big brown eyes. She didn't say or do anything but stared. She was the size of the room. What I remember is that after three seconds I fell asleep. When I awoke in the morning, I looked for her, but she was gone.

I didn't cry myself to sleep again.

My Journey to the Black Madonna

Street Madonna

2 THE BLACK MADONNA

I first heard about the Black Madonna when I was choosing a name for Confirmation in Catholic School. My sister and I were attending St. Luke's School in the South Bronx. The nun told us that we needed a new middle name. She said that many of us were baptized with pagan names. We needed the name of a saint that we wanted to emulate as good Catholics. There was to be a special Church ceremony in which we would be confirmed with our new name. I was having a difficult time deciding on a name so I spoke with Mami after dinner.

"I have to choose a name for confirmation but I don't know what name to pick."

"What is confirmation?"

"Confirmation is like a second baptism. By laying his hands on us in prayer the priest confers the gift of the Holy Spirit on us. The nun said we take a new name because a lot of us were given pagan names at birth. She said my friend's name, Minerva is a pagan name. I like her name, but the nun said Minerva is the name of a pagan goddess. She said we have to pick the name of a Catholic saint for confirmation. She said if we have a pagan name we will go to hell". Mom smirked and thought for a while.

"How about Monserrate. It is after Our Lady of Montserrat. She is a Black Madonna from Puerto Rico who is famous for miracles," she said.

"What kind of miracles?" she asked.

"She heals the sick."

Mom explained that the sickness could be anything. It could be rheumatic fever, heart problems, arthritis, or tuberculosis. People prayed to Our Lady when there were hurricanes. They believed she would protect their homes, families, and animals. There were some serious hurricanes in Puerto Rico. She said people could lose their homes and their lives. They thanked her for the miracles by giving her gold, silver, or wax Milagros. Some thanked her by climbing the one hundred steps to her Sanctuary on their knees. She knelt on the floor and raised her knees one at a time to show us, someone, climbing one step at a time on their knees.

She said they also pinned Milagros to the Madonna's clothing or onto the backcloth of the altar in the

Church. The Black Madonna of Puerto Rico received thousands of Milagros a year.

In Puerto Rico, people only gave Milagros when they received healing.

"I didn't know we had someone famous from Puerto Rico. In class the other day the teacher said we were going to learn about Puerto Rico. I was so excited. I wanted to learn more about where we come from. I couldn't wait to go to school. In school, I waited all day. Towards the end of class, the teacher remembered her promise. She looked at me and asked me to read the chapter on Puerto Rico. The Geography book said that Puerto Rico is a small island in the Caribbean Sea. She pointed it out on the map in front of the classroom and said it is no larger than a dot on the map. The farmers grow sugar cane and ship it to the United States where they process and package it. There was a small black and white photo of a dark bare-chested man swinging a machete in a sugar cane field. He wore soiled pants tied at the waist with a rope. The children in the class looked at me and put their noses up in the air like Puerto Ricans weren't all that. That was the lesson on Puerto Rico." I sat slump-shouldered and sighed.

My mother frowned. She walked into her bedroom and dragged out an old brown suitcase from under her bed. She brought it into the living room and put it on the blue glass coffee table. She opened the snaps and dug inside. There were a lot of papers. She pulled out a newspaper clipping which she held up. It was a picture of a bald heavyset man playing a cello.

"This is Pablo Casals. He is a Puerto Rican musician who lives in San Juan. His mother is Puerto Rican. He played at Carnegie Hall." She dug a little deeper and pulled out a black wood-framed picture of a Black Madonna. "This is La Monserrate."

La Monserrate was a beautiful brown-skinned Madonna with long black hair. She wore a long flowing red gown and on her head a white veil topped with a crown of gold. A group of altar boys dressed in black cassocks and white surplices surrounded her. Behind her, there were tall serrated mountains.

I decided to take Monserrate as my Confirmation name. A miracle-working Madonna from my Island made me feel proud of being Puerto Rican. My mother gave me a porcelain and gold medal of the Black Madonna of Montserrat. It was the only image I had of the Black Madonna from Puerto Rico. I wore it for many years.

3 SERENDIPITY

1991

I was taking a ceramic sculpture class at the Garrison Art Center in Cold Spring New York. The students were seated on stools around wooden tables set up with clay and wooden clay tools. Facing the teacher, we could see outside the windows. We could see and hear the water of the Hudson River swiping against the shore.

"What do you want to work on?" Siglinda asked us.

"I want to make a relief sculpture of Our Lady of Montserrat," I said. "She is a Black Madonna famous for miracles in Puerto Rico. I took that name for confirmation. I had a beautiful gold and porcelain medal of her. Thieves took it when they robbed my apartment in Manhattan."

"We have a Black Madonna in Italy that is famous for miracles," Siglinda said to my surprise.

"I didn't know there were Black Madonnas in Italy. In Catholic School, I learned there were only Black Madonnas in places where the people were black. The nun said the Madonna looked like the people."

"I don't think that is the case in Italy," Siglinda said. She had dark brown hair and alabaster-colored skin.

She played Italian opera music while we worked on our projects. That day the radio announcer said, "This weekend there is a new opera at the Cathedral of St. John the Divine in Manhattan. It is "Il Viaggio di La Madonna Nera," the Voyage of the Black Madonna by the Belloni Cantata." Siglinda and I stared at each other.

"Do you want to go?" she asked me.

"Yes."

"I want to go too," a student in the class blurted out.

"Me too," chimed in another student.

"It sounds like we have a field trip to the opera," Siglinda smiled.

That weekend we shared a potluck dinner at the home of one of the students in Cold Spring. We feasted green salad from one of the student's gardens and fruit salad with cantaloupe and juicy watermelon. I brought a Tabbouleh salad with tomatoes and olive oil and lemon. After dinner, we carpooled to the Cathedral of St. John the Divine in Manhattan. Paintings of the Black Madonna surrounded the stage. They were dark-skinned icons of the Black Madonna and child. Their appearance was regal, their clothes and crowns golden. The operetta was in Italian. Siglinda translated for us. It was a good thing we were sitting in the rear. I learned that in Italy the people make pilgrimages to the Black Madonna on her feast day. They carry her statue on a small boat which they send out to sea. In the operetta, they showed her rescuing those who prayed to her during storms at sea.

I finished my bas relief sculpture of Our Lady of Montserrat at the art center. It was ceramic and the Madonna assumed a throne position. Her skin was brown and she had a long nose that protruded from the image. She wore a red robe and a gold crown. I used gold paint on the crown and the cross held by Jesus. I attached semi-precious stones of amethyst and quartz to the crown and the cross. She held a white lily. I framed the image in six-inch square mosaic tiles of gray and royal blue that I made. I also made a gray wooden frame to contrast with the tiles. I hung it in my studio at Taller Boricua. A group of artists from Vistas Latinas visited my studio. They loved my Madonna and selected it for the group exhibition at the Hillwood Art Museum. The gallery was a large open space with twenty-foot-high ceilings. They placed my Black Madonna at the entrance to the exhibition.

Stony Brook University

At the opening of the exhibition, I stood near my artwork chatting with my husband and friends. Two white women entered the gallery. They both had blond hair bobbed in a page boy a la Lauren Bacall. They wore matching Lands' End suits in beige. One sported a beige button-down collar blouse and the other a similar one in white. The lady with the beige blouse stared long and hard at my Black Madonna. She pressed very tight to the brown-skinned Madonna's nose with her nose. She took a slight step back.

"She is Black! Why is the Madonna black?" She whispered loud enough for me to hear. I looked. Her friend whispered something in her ear. It calmed the white lady with the beige blouse. I didn't hear what her friend said.

I didn't understand why it was so hard for the lady in beige to see the Madonna as a dark-skinned woman. It reminded me of the many times that I experienced rejection for being Puerto Rican with olive-colored skin.

More Serendipity

A few weeks later I was walking along Sixth Avenue in Greenwich Village browsing the used book tables along the street when I noticed a book titled, The Cult of the Black Virgin. I kept walking, but I backtracked and picked it up. In it Ean Begg, a Jungian Psychologist, documented over 350 images of the Black Madonna around the world. (A reprint of the book 10 years later documented 450 Black Madonnas.) I used the Gazetteer at the end of his book to locate the Black Madonna in Puerto Rico, Mexico, Spain, Italy, China, Portugal and France.

Monserrat bas-relief sculpture

4 THE ENGLISH PAPER

1963

My family moved to Union City, New Jersey. My aunt Gilda and Irish Uncle Jimmy were living there. Aunt Gilda encouraged us to move nearby because there was less crime than in the Bronx where we lived.

My mother and German stepfather Jack went apartment hunting. In the first interview, the building manager said to my mother, "I notice you have an accent. Where are you from?"

"Puerto Rico," she replied.

"You don't look Puerto Rican," he smiled.

They did not call back about the apartment. My stepfather called them after a couple of days. The secretary told him the apartment was rented. My stepfather went apartment hunting alone. He got an apartment the same day.

My mother registered us at St. Michaels. Aunt Gilda attended St. Michael's Church and she told us they were the best school in the area. I attended High School, and my sister went to the elementary school, which was across the street. On the first day of class, I waited outside the school. I felt very alone amid the excited chatter of all the students who knew each other from Freshman year. I was a Sophomore. Looking across the street, I saw my sister, Peggy also looks around a little lost. A couple of girls approached her, and they started talking. Peggy was very talkative and sociable. I was very shy.

Then, two tall girls approached me.

"Hi, you're new here. What's your name?" One of the tall girls asked.

"Elaine Soto," I said.

"Where are you from?" the second-tall girl asked.

"I'm from New York."

"I mean you have an accent."

"I am Puerto Rican."

"Puerto R-i-ican. You don't look Puerto R-i-ican."

Ignoring her companion's remark, the other tall girl said, "I'm Fran and this is Linda."

Then, the school bell rang. Fran smiled at me and she and Linda walked away arm in arm.

I went to my homeroom class; where I discovered that I was on the secretarial studies track. The only other Latino in the school, a Cuban male, was also there. I was hoping this was temporary, but after a couple of days in the class, I realized this was a permanent placement. It was not what I wanted. I was programmed by my mother to go to college and I wanted to fulfill that dream for both of us. I pushed myself to speak with the teacher.

"Sister, I am in the wrong class. I don't want to become a secretary; I want to go to College".

"What is your name?"

"Elaine Soto."

She looked at her roster and said, "You are in the right class." She turned her head and shuffling papers on her desk dismissed me.

Frustrated, I sat down. I discussed it with my mother that evening. She was indignant. Her dream was that we attend college because Grandpa did not encourage the girls to get an education. The next day, my mother went to school with me. She was toting my report cards and medals of Honor from the

Academy and Cathedral High School. The principal said, "That is one of the top ten Catholic Schools in the country." She switched me to the academic track the same day.

In my new English class, I found an empty seat and sat down. Sister Camille, the teacher stared at me and said, "You are new in this class."

"I was in secretarial studies, but they transferred me because I am on the academic track. I plan to go to college."

With an unwelcoming smirk, she said, "This is an Honors English class. I expect you to keep up. Sit there."

I sat down at the end of the second row where she pointed.

Sister Camille spoke about all the exciting activities available at the school. She told us to take advantage of all the opportunities available to us. She encouraged us to join the debating club. She said she was the faculty advisor. It sounded like a good group to join to learn to express myself better. Sister Camille then gave a lesson on the use of metaphors. Our first assignment was a paper utilizing the concept.

Walking home on Kennedy Boulevard, I ran into Fran, the friendly tall girl.

"Hi. I met you on the first day of class," she said.

"Yes, I remember you."

"When did you move to Union City?"

"We moved here last month. We lived in the Bronx. Before my mother remarried, my sister and I lived in a Catholic boarding school in North Haledon."

"I was born and raised in Union City. I went to grammar school across the street from St. Michael's. I'm an Honor student and a cheerleader for the varsity football team," she said in a gush of words.

"Seriously! I was an Honor student at Cathedral High School and a cheerleader in a boarding school for three years. My sister is attending the grammar school across the street."

"What did you think of Sister Camille?" she asked.

"I don't like her. She doesn't think I can do the work of an Honors English class. I was an Honor student at Cathedral High School. I don't know if this is harder." We walked together and shared our experiences with cheerleading, school, and boys. I did not know much about boys. The boarding school was all girls and Cathedral High School was all girls. We arrived at a small two-story brick house and Fran stopped.

"This is my house; would you like to come in? My mother always prepares a snack for me when I get home from school."

"Sure."

Fran looked like her mother. She was tall, thin, with pale white skin. Her nose was long, and she had shoulder-length brown hair. Looking me over, she said, "Welcome."

"Mom, this is Elaine. She is in my English class. Her family moved here from New York."

"Good to meet you, Elaine. I am Rebecca. Welcome to Union City! Please help yourself with some chocolate chip cookies. They are hot from the oven. I'll leave you two to talk. I am preparing dinner."

***

That night I pulled out my old Webster's Dictionary and my new Roget's Thesaurus. My mother bought the dictionary for me at the A&P supermarket when we lived in the Bronx. They sold the dictionary in sections. Mami bought the next section every month. I loved my dictionary, I read each section as soon as my mother brought it home. I sat down at my desk to write. I couldn't write.

My sister blasted the television in the living room. My mother was cooking dinner and listening to the radio in the kitchen.

"Please lower the volume. I'm trying to study," I said, shifting unable to get comfortable.

They lowered their respective volume, but I was still overreacting to the noise.

My stepfather Jack came home from work in the butcher shop. He was talking in a deep tone about his job. They fired a butcher that day without warning. He ranted about it until we sat down for dinner. After dinner, I tried to write, but I was still having trouble. I took a nap. At two in the morning, I got up and gathered my dictionary, thesaurus, encyclopedia, and a lamp, and sat on the floor. Pulling my blanket around me to warm up, I organized my books. I reviewed them and played around with the concept of metaphor. That day my writing muse visited me for the very first time. She inspired me to write about different types of snakes. I researched the various types of snakes in my encyclopedia. Then I likened how they shed their skin to how I felt moving to a new place. It felt like I was shedding my old life skin for a new one living in New Jersey. I pulled the paper together in a couple of hours and went to sleep. The next day I handed it to Sister Camille.

A few days later Sister Camille began our class by saying, "I am very impressed by the papers from this group." Her pale flat face was impassive. As she handed out papers to eager outstretched hands, she said, "One paper was exceptional." Holding the paper up, she looked around the classroom. She walked over to me and said, "Would you read your paper to the class?"

Surprised, I walked to the front of the classroom. I never stood in front of a class to read before. Looking up, I saw Fran smiling at me, but everyone else looked quizzical. My hands quivered and my knees shook. It was hard to read. Thank God the shaking stopped after I read the first page. When I finished reading, the class murmured a single audible sigh. Pleased, I looked up.

Sister Camille bounded up to the front of the classroom and said, "That paper was excellent. Who wrote it for you?"

"No one wrote it for me."

With an incredulous stare, she snarled, "Sit down."

I walked down the aisle to my seat. Fran looked at me. Most of the students averted their eyes.

When I told my mother what happened, her nostrils flared. She came to the parent-teacher conference the following week. She was again toting my honor pins and report cards from the Academy and Cathedral. She met with several teachers and told them about my work and honors and what Sister Camille did. Someone must have warned Sister Camille that an irate parent was looking for her. She disappeared. She never said anything like that to me again.

I did not join the debating club.

5 COLLEGE

1966

I walked into the registrar's office at Monroe High School. The clerk at the desk ignored me. I cleared my throat and said, "Excuse Me." She looked up.

"Can I help you?"

"I need a copy of my High School transcripts. I am applying for college and I need a copy of my transcripts for the application."

She looked at me with a smirk on her lips. Then lips pressing into a white slash she glanced through some files and said. I don't have any transcripts in your file. What school did you say you went to?"

"I went to three High Schools, Cathedral, St. Michael's, and La Escuela Superior de Bayamon in Puerto Rico."

"No transcripts here. Come back next week to see if they came," she said walking away.

I returned the following week and got the same answer. The third week when I returned, I was under pressure because the application was due. The clerk again looked through the files and said the same thing.

As I was leaving a pretty brown-skinned woman who observed our interaction asked, "What do you need?"

"I need a copy of my transcripts. It is three weeks and it isn't in my file yet. My application for City College is due this week."

The clerk walked out of the room shrugging. The pretty brown-skinned lady stared at her back and smirked. She dug into the files, found mine, and pulled out the transcripts. She copied them and gave me copies. She signed the Monroe transcript. She was Ms. Santos, the school guidance counselor.

I was accepted at City College. I chose to attend Baruch, the Business School downtown. I didn't know what I wanted to study only that Mami wanted me to attend college. She encouraged me to study hard and to get good grades and I did. She taught me to "reach for the moon". I did that too, but I didn't know what I was reaching for in college. I was the first one to go to college in my family. When I spoke with the Guidance Counselor at Monroe, he asked what my mother did for a living. I told him she was a Hairdresser and that she owned Martin's Beauty Salon on Boynton Avenue. His eyes lit up and he suggested a business school, Baruch College. I didn't know what to expect so I learned about College as I went along.

The English Teacher

Mr. Murphy was my English teacher at Baruch. I tried to write a paper for class, but I was stuck. Nothing came out. He asked me to drop by his office. When I arrived, he was on his way to a meeting, but he made time to speak with me.

"Elaine, you said you are having trouble writing. What is the matter?" He sat in front of an old Royal typewriter perched on an oak desk piled high with books and papers.

"I don't know. I have trouble sitting down to write. When I finally sit down to write, nothing comes out."

"Has it always been like this for you? You have to be an excellent student because Baruch accepted you. I couldn't look at him. I felt upset.

"I love to write."

"Did something happen to make you stop loving it?"

"Yes. I attended a Catholic school in Union City New Jersey. On my first day in the English class, the teacher asked me my name and when I told her she said,

"This is an Honors class. I expect you to keep up."

"I felt like she didn't think I could do it." She gave us the assignment to work on a paper using a metaphor.

I wrote it and she asked me to read it in front of the class. When I finished reading, she asked who wrote it for me. After that, I couldn't sit down to write.

"Hum. I see." He shook his white-haired head.

He asked me to sit down in front of his big Royal typewriter and said. "When I have trouble writing, what I do is sit down in front of the typewriter and type anything that comes to mind. My name, a few words, whatever comes. Once I do that whatever I need to write comes to me. I would like you to try it. I have a short meeting, but I will be back. Please sit here and write the story you told me." I sat down and looked at the blank paper in the typewriter. I got up and went to the bathroom. I came back. I stared at the paper. I typed my name. As I typed the story of what happened in the English class flowed from me. I wrote about the humiliation I felt in front of the class. I wrote about how embarrassed I felt when people looked away as I walked down the aisle to my seat. I wrote about not joining the debating club. Mr. Murphy returned and asked me to read my paper out loud. I did and I cried. He listened and at the end, he gave me his white handkerchief.

"You'll feel better now," he said.

I did and my writing got better. I joined Ticker, the Baruch College Newspaper, and I became a reporter. A year later I became Associate Editor. I joined PRIDE (Puerto Ricans for Involvement,

Development, and Enlightenment). I also learned how to dance Salsa.

6 LOOKING FOR MY FATHER

Mami I want to see my father

I don't know why you want to see that son of a bitch

Sometimes I think I could be sitting next to him on the train

And not know it is my father

I don't know why you want to see that son of a bitch

He never supported you

And not know it is my father

Her two eyes twitched at once

He never supported you

He left when the judge ruled he had to pay child support

Her two eyes twitched at once

He never sent you a birthday card or a present

He left when the judge ruled he had to pay child support

I loved him but I couldn't tell her

He never sent you a birthday card or a present

She had a thought disorder when it came to my father

I loved him but I couldn't tell her

I kept quiet

She had a thought disorder when it came to my father

It took everything I had to speak now

I kept quiet

Her eyes welled up and she left the room

It took everything I had to speak now

She ignored me for two weeks

Her eyes welled up and she left the room

She averted her face and her body stiffened

She ignored me for two weeks

Then she left a letter propped up on my desk

She averted her face and her body stiffened

I avoided her too

Then she left a letter propped up on my desk

I don't understand why you want to see your father

I avoided her too

I feared her rage

I don't know why you want to see your father

You can put an ad in El Diario La Prensa and his family might tell him

I feared her rage

I survived being silent

You can put an ad in El Diario La Prensa and his family might tell him

I felt her love

Elaine Soto

I survived being silent

Mami I want to see my father

I felt her love

Sometimes I think I could be sitting next to him on the train

1974

"I am going to Puerto Rico to look for our father. Mom said his family is from Santa Isabel near Ponce." I was on the phone talking with my sister, Peggy.

"God, you're thinking about him too."

"Yeah, I keep thinking I could be sitting next to him on the train and not even know I was sitting next to my father."

"I know what you mean. I often wonder what happened to him. I am glad you are looking for him."

I flew to Puerto Rico. I rented a car at the San Juan airport and drove to Mayaguez. When I arrived in Mayaguez, my uncle Sam insisted on accompanying me. He said it was dangerous for a woman to travel alone in Puerto Rico. Together we drove south to Ponce and then east to Santa Isabel, my father's hometown. In the middle of town, we stopped at a cafetín, a small coffee shop and my uncle Sam inquired about the Soto family. The first person we asked said he didn't know them. An older man sitting at the counter drinking coffee turned around and looked at us. "I know them." He directed us to a small green wood frame house a couple of blocks away from the center of town.

I knocked on the wooden door. A thin, gray-haired woman answered. She wore a white blouse with pink flowers and a gray skirt past her knees. She had an olive complexion and high cheekbones like mine. Her hair was short and combed back away from her face. She was a very pretty older woman. Her square jaw and high cheekbones spoke of a once very attractive woman. She had a lovely smile that reminded me of my sister's smile. I introduced myself and told her I was looking for my father.

"Chu doesn't live here. He lives in Chicago," she said and paused. "Israel, his brother is here. He can tell you where he is."

"Oh, I know Israel. When I was a little girl, he visited us in Manhattan."

"He went to the bodega. Wait for him. He will be right back. Would you like a cup of coffee while you wait?"

"I would love it," I said excited to see my uncle again. As Sam and I drank coffee, she scanned my face. She told me she did not see my father since he moved to Chicago. He called her sometimes. She took me into her small bedroom and showed me the back wall where she had a gallery of pictures. There was a picture of my grandfather who had straight black hair combed straight back. On his face, he wore a foreboding look. There was a very handsome black-haired man in an army uniform. My grandmother said he was her oldest son who died in the war. He looked a lot like my father. He was dark and handsome with black hair and mustache, and a long nose. Next, there was a picture of my pretty aunt, Rosa. She had dark hair and eyes, and she sat alone in a rose garden. There was a picture of my father with uncle Israel. They posed in a photography studio rendition of driving in a convertible. I took pictures of the pictures. I realized that I looked a lot like my father's family. My olive complexion and dark hair and eyes were definitely from his side of the family. I even had a space in my front teeth like my uncle Israel. When my uncle Israel returned from the bodega, he was very happy to see me. He said he was going to Chicago to visit my father next week and he would let him know that I was looking for him. I gave him my phone number.

A week later, a sexy voiced man called. It was my father. It was like a field of lavender father flowers. I knew he loved me even though my mother said he didn't. She worked hard at separating us, but I still loved him like the smell of Lavender. He loved that we wanted to see him. He bought two plane tickets to Chicago for me and my sister. We were very excited, but we both felt guilty about looking for him. We knew Mami would be angry when she found out. My father was still very tall and handsome, but his hair was thinning on top. I spotted him right away in the crowd at O'Hare airport. He wore a long dark overcoat. The same coat I often saw him wearing in my dreams. My sister's face was identical to his but younger. It was like they took his face and pasted it on her. It was amazing. My mother didn't lie about her looking like him. My hands were also identical to his. My mother always said I had long fingers and nails like my father. My skin color was also like his, olive. She told the truth about that too. He smiled and hugged me and Peggy with gusto when we approached him. His eyes sparkled with affection when he looked at me. I saw in his eyes that he loved me.

His wife and my two stepbrothers were also waiting. She was petite with cinnamon color skin and black hair and eyes. The boys were a combination of my father and their mother. One was tall and had an olive complexion with dark hair and eyes like my father. The younger one was short and had cinnamon color skin like his mother. The younger one was very happy to meet us, and he kept making jokes to make us laugh. The older one was quiet and aloof.

Papi took us around Chicago to see the sights like the famous Lake Shore Drive. It was very cold in Chicago and he bought us warm pants and a sweater to keep us warm. Chicago is the home of the hawk. It is colder than New York. His wife was kind and happy to get to know us. She prepared arroz con gandules, tostones, and steak for dinner. We had a good time joking, laughing, taking pictures and dancing. He played mambo, merengue, and bolero music. We all danced. He had some very old records from Puerto Rico. He loved music and he was eager to share it with us. He played Rafael Hernandez's "En mi Viejo San Juan". It brought tears to his eyes.

Later, when we had a private moment to talk, I asked him why he wasn't faithful to Mami. "Yo era bonito"

I was handsome, he said. He was. I remembered. My sister, Peggy, who was identical to him was also very pretty. The man who talked to me now was still handsome, but he wasn't as tall as I remembered him.

While we were dancing he excused himself to go to the restroom several times. A short while after, I went to the bathroom. As I walked down the long dark hallway, I passed a pantry and I startled Papi who was hiding inside. He was sneaking a drink from a bottle of Bacardi rum. He hid it behind the rice and canned gandules on the top shelf. He put his finger to his lips and opened his eyes wide. He said his wife didn't want him to drink. He offered me a slug and he took another. We returned to the living room and danced. We had fun, but he danced a little too close to me.

He called me a few times after our visit. Each time it was after midnight and I could hear old Puerto Rican love songs playing in the background. I didn't understand a lot of what he was saying. He slurred his speech. I bought him a father's day card. But I didn't mail it.

7 PUERTO RICO

Long braids flowing down my back
First trip in search of the Black Madonna
The miracle worker of Puerto Rico
Our Lady of Montserrat in Hormigueros

First trip in search of the Black Madonna
Camera ready to record it all
Our Lady of Montserrat in Hormigueros
Sam, my uncle, accompanied me

Camera ready to record it all
The quest started with "Why is the Madonna Black?"

My Journey to the Black Madonna

Sam, my uncle, accompanied me

Nan, my husband, was there too

The quest started with "Why is the Madonna Black?"

Vistas Latinas Art Exhibit at Stony Brook University

Nan, my husband, was there too

In Hormigueros she sat tall dressed in pink

Vistas Latinas Art Exhibit at Stony Brook University

Long braids flowing down my back

In Hormigueros she sat tall dressed in pink

The miracle worker of Puerto Rico

Hormigueros Puerto Rico

1992

Hormigueros is on the southwest corner of the Island of Puerto Rico. The church is on top of a small hill on la Calle Monserrate. We parked the car and climbed up 100 concrete steps to the church entrance. Each of the steps was a foot high. I tried climbing a couple of them on my knees to see how it felt. Brutal. The concrete was a high reach and very rough on my knobby knees. My mother visited Hormigueros during Holy Week. She said the worshippers carried the Black Madonna outside in a procession. Some climbed the one hundred steps to the church on their knees. Dona Aleja did this many years ago to thank the Madonna for healing her son who was dying. An artist friend shared that his mother also climbed the steps on her knees. She was thanking the Madonna for healing him of scarlet fever.

Inside the Church on the right is the chapel of St. Rose of Lima. Rafael Colon Morales, a Puerto Rican artist in New York told me about St. Rose of Lima. He said she was a Puerto Rican nun. The Dominican order sent her to Lima, Peru, where she became famous for her asceticism and help of the needy. Above the altar is a painting of the Virgin of Montserrat by Jose Campeche. The priests used the gold from melted Milagros given to the Madonna to make this frame. Campeche was a Puerto Rican artist who studied in France. He returned to Puerto Rico to live and paint. Looking at the rear of the church on the left, I saw a beautiful brown-skinned Madonna. She sat on a mahogany carrier and she held a brown baby in her arms. She had a powerful presence. Her hair was long and black and styled in banana curls that flowed down her back. She and the baby wore rose-colored garments.

Before going to Puerto Rico, I read several books about the Black Madonna of Montserrat. I was an Artist in Residence at Taller Boricua and worked painting in my studio in El Barrio. For the first image of La Monserrate, I went to Botanica Justo on 104th Street. It is a religious articles store. There I found a print like the one my mother had. I used the image on the print to paint my first Black Madonna. I made it door size and in mixed media. La Monserrate has been famous for miracles since the 18th Century. People came from all over the Island to hang Milagros on her gown. I copied the Milagros given to her. I used images in the book Los Milagros en Cera y en Metal de Puerto Rico by Teodoro Vidal. He said that in Puerto Rico the giving of Milagros was an offering for healings received. The Catholic Church banned the practice of giving Milagros in 1954. This was the year after Puerto Rico had its very own Marian Apparition. La Virgen Del Rosario appeared to three young children in the town of Sabana Grande. When I told my artist friend, Diogenes, that I was going to Puerto Rico to find La Monserrate. He said I had to visit Sabana Grande.

My Journey to the Black Madonna

Hormigueros Monserrate

Elaine Soto

Monserrate with Milagros

Sabana Grande

We drove to Sabana Grande. There, a ten-foot-tall statue of the Madonna dressed in white with a blue cloak greeted us. A ring of seven stars surrounded her head like a crown. Our Lady of the Rosary appeared aloft a tree to three school children in El Barrio Rincon of Sabana Grande. She appeared to them for thirty-three consecutive days from April 23 to May 25, 1953. The children were Juan Angel Collado, and Isidra and Ramonita Belen. Their ages were 7, 8, and 9 years old. They were students at the small red schoolhouse. At lunchtime, their task was to get water from a nearby well. The Blessed Mother appeared for the first time to Juan Angel when he went to get water from the well. There was a profound silence and he saw her. She seemed to be standing aloft a cloud near the well. A white tunic and a blue mantle clothed her. In her hands, she held a rosary and a crown of seven stars hovered above her head. Her face resembled that of a beautiful Puerto Rican woman. She had a tan complexion and black hair and eyes.

During that time, a lot of people came to visit the apparition site. Not everyone could see the Madonna. Some people reported that there was a shower of rain in the colors of the rainbow. Then the sun came out and whirled around the sky. The newspapers called it the "Miracle of the Sun". Thousands of miracles and healings took place during her apparition. She left 7 prophesies with Juan Angel Collado. She instructed him on the appropriate timing for their revelation.

Four of the prophesies follow:

1. Call your mother for help on the way to God and during times of turmoil.

2. Be an apostle-a light of this time it is a very difficult time. Get protection under her mantel and virtues. From 1953 onward there will be seven generations and no more. Construct and follow the path of plenitude.

3. It is the hour for all to become the Voice of the Way. Spread charity by your words and by your example. A great danger threatens humanity. I promise to give protection under my mantel. I will help all those who in these difficult moments, pray five mysteries of the rosary every day.

4. It is the hour in which the prophecies will fulfill because you have not heeded my warnings. One day the vault of heaven will be orange at dawn. There will be an intense cold. Great tribulation and desperation will fall over humanity. It will be as if hell settled on earth. Parents, children, and all human beings will want to kill each other. They will fight with each other till death. The skin of some men will fall and drip over their bones. Others will become monstrous and abominable beings and they will behave like demons. If the chosen become converted and start living a life dedicated to prayer. If these apostles fast, abstain, and mortify the senses, they will lead the way to the plenitude of my Son.

These prophecies were revealed from 1987 to 1992. For later revelations visit: http://virgendelpozo.org.

The Miracle of the Sun

The cashier working in the gift shop shared that she saw the second "Miracle of the Sun" in 1990. She said she thought the first apparition was an "old wives' tale". But when she saw the second Miracle of the Sun, she believed that the Madonna appeared in 1953. She said that during the second Miracle of the Sun, it rained, and the raindrops were in the colors of the rainbow. There is a video documenting the event for sale in the gift shop. A couple of family friends who lived in Patillas saw the Miracle of the Sun in 1990. Julio and Sabita reported that they were at the pilgrimage site that day.

Sabita said, "I was praying the rosary with everyone outside when it started to rain with the sun shining. Everyone became a different color. I became green and Julio became red. The sun revolved around its orbit in the sky." Sabita gave me a beautiful blue crystal rosary from Sabana Grande. I started praying the rosary after I read the Madonna's prophecies.

When we visited the apparition site. A gate surrounded the tree where the Madonna appeared aloft a cloud. There was an underground stream that erupted on the spot. The water healed those who drank it with faith. It is now accessible through a spigot outside the gate. Near the site, there was a casita containing Milagros to the Virgin for healing received. There was a wide assortment of Milagros. There were ex-votos and pictures of people and saints and letters of thanks propped up on a table. There were statues of saints. There were bridal gowns, baby clothes, and military uniforms. There were dolls and toys, and prosthetic devices, crutches, and a wheelchair. The water healed a paralyzed artist. Her wheelchair sits there as testimony.

Close to the apparition site, it was dark, silent, and still. A coqui, a Puerto Rican tree frog sang "coqui, coqui, coqui" breaking the silence. As I stood there, stillness and strong energy filled my body and made me feel like crying.

Taller Boricua

I was sitting on the stoop in front of the Taller Boricua studio building on 106th Street. Roberto, a Puerto Rican poet stopped by to visit. He was medium height and weight and he wore a gray newsboy cap over his brown hair. He greeted me with a smile and climbed up the steps and sat down a step below me. I was taking a break from painting. I loved sitting there on my breaks and absorbing the energy of El Barrio. Irma, the Administrative Director of the Taller encouraged him to come over and talk to me. Since I am a Psychologist, she often referred people who were sad or distressed to talk to me. Roberto was sad. He had lost his wife three months earlier. He shared his regrets about not having sex with her the day she died. She asked him to have sex, but he was in a hurry to get to work and left. She died that day of a heart attack. Tears rolled down his cheeks as he shared the story.

While we were talking, a couple of men from the Church next door lugged out a 6-foot wooden panel with an arched top. They laid it next to the garbage cans on the side of the stoop where Roberto and I were sitting.

"That would make great support for my Madonna painting. It looks heavy. I wish I could carry it up to my studio," I said.

"I'll help you carry it," he said. We both lifted the wooden panel and carried it to the landing of the stoop. It was very heavy and long and we had to maneuver a lot to get it up the narrow staircase of the three-story brownstone. Stopping for air at each landing, we carried it up to my third-floor studio.

Later that day I primed the wooden panel with gesso. I painted the Madonna in Noelle Méndez de Guzmán's book, La Verdadera Historia de la Aparición de la Virgen Del Rosario. It was at the end of his book. I called the painting "La Virgen del Pozo". A couple of days later when I was meditating, I saw an image of the Madonna behind a veil with one eye. I painted it. It is "Behind the Veil".

From here on I followed the lead of early icon painters. They used natural materials like egg tempera and encaustic to paint sacred images. They believed that natural material connected to the energy of the Madonna or saint. I started using encaustic, which my friend Diogenes taught me.

Virgen del Pozo

My Journey to the Black Madonna

Behind the Veil

Virgen del Barrio

In 1994 I was practicing a Course in Miracles, by the Foundation for Inner Peace. It is a simple self-study program to awaken to oneness with God and Love. I was repeating the mantra for the day. It was "The past is over; it can hurt me not." That evening I was praying and looking at a night light I had next to my bed. The light had the image of the Madonna in white plastic. I went to sleep and in a dream, I saw the Madonna. She was beautiful with tan skin and she had her hand on her heart which was afire. In the background, there were old abandoned buildings. They were like the ones in the South Bronx where I grew up and survived a difficult childhood. She stood afloat near the building and looked at me. Inside myself, I heard the words "the past is over, it can hurt me not." The next day I decided to paint that Madonna. I needed a beautiful Puerto Rican woman as a model. I asked Irma for permission to photograph her face for my painting. She agreed. I used her face for the Madonna. I also used the image of some old abandoned buildings in El Barrio. They were like the buildings in the South Bronx where I grew up. I collaged the words "The past is over; it can hurt me not" to her heart. I called the painting "La Virgen Del Barrio".

Virgen del Barrio

8 CHINA

In 1995 I went to the Fourth World Conference on Women in China. There were one hundred women artists from the College Art Association. I traveled with another visual artist named Cromo. She is a petite, dark-haired woman from Peru. She is very pretty and sports a beauty mark on her left cheek. She was a nurse. We met at a meeting in the Ceres Gallery in SoHo for the Women's Caucus for Art. We were all seated in folding chairs in the middle of the gallery floor. They discussed an upcoming trip to China for which they needed presenters. I didn't consider volunteering because I didn't have extra money to go to China. I told Cromo and she said to me "save." We can save enough money in a year to go. I can present on nursing and art in the Queens Community. You can present on the Black Madonna and expressive art groups in El Barrio. She convinced me and we planned the trip together. We found reasonable flights to China and Russia. We included Russia via the trans-Siberian railroad. I

wanted to visit the Hermitage i.
Russia. We traveled there after the (

For the Conference, we flew to Shai.
Airlines. It was a fifteen-hour trip. The
and snacks every couple of hours. 1
socks to keep our feet warm, and warm ..nd towels
to wash our hands. We joined the one hundred
women at the designated hotel in Shanghai. They
drove us in a school bus cross country from Shanghai
to Beijing, where the conference was being held. The
bus drove along routes sanctioned by the Chinese
government. We visited beautiful parks with
fountains and lotus-filled ponds. There was a special
one with outdoor sculptures of Chinese Buddha
carved into the rock wall. I took early morning walks.
I observed groups of Chinese people doing Tai Chi
in the parks. The tour drove us to clay factories where
they sold beautiful handmade teapots. We also
visited stores where they sold jewelry made of jade
and pearls. They even had creams made from pearls
which brightened and beautified the skin. I didn't
buy those, but many women in the group surrounded
the shop counters buying them. What I did buy were
paint, paint brushes, and paper for future art projects.
Cromo helped me pick out the best brushes for the
price. She was savvy that way.

We wanted to meet with some of the Chinese artists
in Beijing, but they were hesitant. After we tried to
set up a meeting with them, the green police started
to watch us. I was in my hotel room preparing my
presentation. A light green uniformed policeman

...d my door and walked in. I was sitting on my ...d and looked up. He excused himself and left. Later, Cromo and I found the things in our suitcases shifted around. Nothing was missing, but we knew they were checking us out. We never met with the Beijing artists. Before we went on the trip, the Women's Caucus for Art leaders warned us not to mention Tibet. They were not permitting anyone to visit there. I would have loved to visit the home of the Dalai Lama. They told us if we got caught going there, the authorities would immediately put us on a plane and send us home. They said there was nothing they could do to help us if that happened.

On the trip, I became aware of the Goddess Guan Yin, a Bodhisattva which I saw in several Buddhist temples. A Bodhisattva is an enlightened person or Buddha who chooses to stay on the earth plane. They chose to help humanity instead of leaving when they achieve enlightenment. Guan Yin is the goddess of Compassion and Mercy. In my research, I found a legend about her and I used it to paint her image when I came home.

The legend is that the son of the king of the sea wanted to go out and play in the ocean. He assumed the form of a carp. As he was swimming about in the ocean, he didn't notice fishermen's nets and he got caught in them. He cried out for help, and Guan Yin heard his cries and rescued him. She holds a vase with a sacred healing balm which she uses to bless and heal. It is symbolic of her role as "she who hears the cries of the world as wisdom". Saying this mantra honors her and brings her closer to us. When I returned from China, I painted Guan Yin riding on the back of a large carp. It is a large painting in encaustic and is 55 inches high by 55 inches wide.

On another occasion, while I was meditating saying her mantra I saw her. I felt like a bolt of energy. Then I saw her in the woods behind my home in Peekskill New York. She was walking in the woods accompanied by a yellow tiger. I painted this image on a very large canvas, 6 feet high by 8 feet wide in encaustic. The image is of a luscious green forest. In it, a beautiful Chinese woman dressed in white holds a vase for healing. I used the beautiful face of a Chinese tour guide named Ping.

Guan Yin

Tiananmen Square

Beijing

Another artist from New York and I went to dinner near Tiananmen Square. They had a three-story McDonald's packed with Chinese people. We entered and ordered fish fillets, fries, and cokes. The McDonalds was like the ones in New York golden arch and all. After dinner, we walked across the street to the Square. Tiananmen Square is known for the crackdown on student protests in 1989. Troops advanced on the pro-democracy demonstrators and bystanders and arrested 10,000. They executed several dozens for their part in the demonstrations. That night it was quiet and there were a few people walking about. There was an older lady with a long beige coat walking with a young boy. He was about five years old and was on roller skates. My gray-haired friend sported a jean jacket embellished with a variety of metal pins. They were souvenirs from her many travels. She had several pins which she collected on our tour through China on the front of her jacket. The little boy skated over to her and stood gazing at her pins. My friend looked at him and smiled. The boy was cute with straight black hair and an engaging smile. She looked at a pin he was admiring and unclasped it. She pinned it on his beige windbreaker. He smiled at her and skated back to his guardian who was walking over to us.

Military police wearing dark green uniforms and carrying guns intercepted them. They looked at the boy's jacket and the pin and looked back at us. My friend smiled at them, but they didn't smile back. They walked away talking to them.

My friend looked at me and said, "It's a good thing I gave him a pin from China."

Green Tara

My friend and I went shopping in small shops near the Conference Center. I found a beautiful Thangka painting of Green Tara. I didn't have enough money to buy it, but my friend offered to lend it to me. I used the Thangka as a reference image for my encaustic painting of Green Tara when I returned to my studio.

I was painting in my studio. I was angry with my mother. She offered my apartment to relatives as a place to stay without discussing it with me. I raised my paintbrush to apply paint on the wood panel when I felt an electrical charge surge through my body. With it came a nonverbal message, "Forgive her, she doesn't know better."

My Journey to the Black Madonna

Green Tara

9 MONTSERRAT SPAIN

Plodding up a curvy mountain road

At the top, a multitude moving to and fro

Some in bridal dresses looking for blessings

Others in wheelchairs praying for healing

At the top, a multitude moving to and fro

It grew from a small church into a massive Basilica

Others in wheelchairs praying for healing

They knelt before the miracle-working Black Madonna

It grew from a small church into a massive Basilica

Mosaics of Catherine of Sienna and Hildegard Van Bingen

They knelt before the miracle-working Black Madonna

"One is not well married until one visits Montserrat."

Mosaics of Catherine of Sienna and Hildegard Van Bingen

Cover the walls leading to her bejeweled chapel

"One is not well married until one visits Montserrat."

Mary Magdalene preaching

Cover the walls leading to her bejeweled chapel

Some in bridal dresses looking for blessings

Mary Magdalene preaching

Plodding up a curvy mountain road

Monastery at Montserrat

My Journey to the Black Madonna

La Moreneta

1994

Montserrat is 25 miles NW of Barcelona on top of a small mountain in Manresa. At the entrance to the monastery, we asked a National Guardsman where we could find the Black Madonna. "La Moreneta?" he asked puzzled. It sounded right, although I had never heard her called that, she was Morena, dark-skinned. I nodded yes and he pointed to the Basilica up ahead. Before we went to the Basilica we registered at El Hotel Abat Cisneros. It is a hotel run by the monastery. We rented a quaint, clean room with two ascetic single beds and a no-frills bathroom with an old sink and a shower.

After a nap, we descended to the church. It was 6 pm and there was brisk rain falling. We waited a while for it to stop. When we arrived at the Church, it was empty. As we walked on the right-hand side of the basilica we passed several large stained glass windows. The window closest to the Black Madonna's chapel showed a wedding scene. In it Jesus put a ring on the finger of a red-haired Mary. A rabbi is blessing the union. The walls along the staircase up to the chapel display mosaics of women saints. Hildegard Van Bingen, St. Catherine of Sienna, and Mary Magdalene. Mary Magdalene has her hands uplifted and is preaching to a group of men. We climbed a few steps to a small chapel. Inside a black-faced Madonna and child sit on a throne. Her smile is subtle and exudes abiding peace. I was so excited to be there that I became stuck in place taking the same picture of the Madonna over and over again. Nan who was standing on the other side of the statue called me. "Come you can get another angle of the statue over here." The five-foot wooden statue encased in glass has a hole in the glass where the Madonna's hand extends. In her hand is a globe. The backdrop is a sheet of gold encrusted with gems and semi-precious stones.

A Benedictine monk walked into the chapel. He looked at us and then prayed. He kissed the Madonna's extended hand. As he left, he fixed his gaze on me and my camera. He smiled as he walked out of the small enclosure. I too kissed the Madonna's hand. I felt the same quiet stillness here that I felt in Sabana Grande. At 6:30 pm the monk returned and scooted us out of the chapel. We left with much reluctance.

Early the next morning we returned. This time there was a long line extending from the entrance of the Basilica to the small chapel. We walked in after waiting for a half-hour. Each person crossed themselves and prayed as they viewed the statue. The space in the chapel was narrow and only a couple of people could view the Madonna at a time. Nan squeezed into a corner on the left and stayed there. I walked to the rear chapel where the back of the statue was visible. The energy here was also powerful.

According to Ean Begg the location of a Black Virgin marks the site of a wouivre or a telluric current. A telluric current is an electric earth current. It moves underground or through the sea. It is an invisible network of energy lines across the earth.

They are a prehistoric track aligning two prominent energetic points in the landscape. The Ancients built Stonehenge, the Great Pyramids, and the Great Wall of China along ley lines. In the 12th Century many Gothic Cathedrals sat on these lines. Chartres Cathedral in France has windows that are lit up at night by the moon at certain times of the year. They had sacred information about astronomy to which we no longer have access. This underground stream is invisible. But sensitives can detect it. It is the flow of our life current and the energy of the cosmos. Often there are streams underground near Black Madonnas. The water from them heals. This is the case in Puerto Rico at Sabana Grande and in Lourdes France.

Nan unglued himself from the Madonna and walked to the rear chapel. I sat there praying the rosary and crying. He patted me on my back. I don't know why I was crying. I wasn't sad when I arrived at the chapel but now I couldn't stop crying. Memories of my father flooded me. Behind me, a Benedictine monk knelt praying the rosary. He looked straight ahead; a silent testament to my tears.

History of Miracles at Montserrat

In 880 seven boys were tending sheep on the mountain. On several Saturdays, they saw a light shining on a cave from the sky. They heard music and songs coming from the cave. They told their parents who told the rector of the parish at Monistrol. The rector observed the light and music until midnight. At that time the light and music ceased and all left in happiness. That Sunday the bishop of the area ordered that they search the location where they saw the vision. When they arrived at the cave there was a wonderful fragrance of roses at the entrance. Inside they found the statue of our lady which is now in the basilica. The bishop at first planned to bring the statue to the town. They carried the Madonna out of the cave, but when they got to a certain point they could not budge the statue. The bishop took this as divine inspiration that they should build a Church on that spot and they did.

The next miracle was in 1239. A retablo depicted the miraculous scene. The image was of someone who was sick in bed. The person prayed to the Virgin and she healed him. The Book of Miracles kept by the Monastery documented hundreds of miracles. In 1323 for example, a drowning sailor invoked Our Lady of Montserrat. She responded: "My son, do not be afraid" and took him by the hand to the shore. In 1520 retablo art depicted that she healed the lame. The healed often climbed the mountain on their knees in offerings of thanks. The list of miracles attributed to our Lady is long. They were freeing prisoners, healing of illnesses, and protection for the injured. They also included helping those followed by vandals, and those given life sentences. She also helped mothers, and in possessions, to the saving of sailors and resurrection of the dead. People gave the virgin ex-votos since the 12th Century as a testimony to a favor received. The ex-votos were the votive photo where they wrote what happened. They were also personal objects like hair, dresses, crutches, orthopedic devices. Some Milagros were wax, wood, and metal reproductions of healed parts. The catalog of ex-votos is diverse. The fire of 1811 destroyed most of the ex-votos up to the 12th Century. Pope Clement III affirmed a history of miracles. We hiked down the mountain to the cave where they found the statue of the Black Madonna. There is a small building that houses the more recent ex-votos.

The fact that she is miraculous is without question at Montserrat. But, the reason for her blackness is without consensus. Anselmo Albareda in his book says her blackness is due to the candle smoke from the small church. Others say she is dark because Mary was a Semite and St. Luke carved her image from life. In one book I read that St. Peter carried the statue to Montserrat and hid it in the cave. Catalonian historians insist that Egyptians brought statues of Isis to Catalonia. The people had a long history of worshipping dark, earthy mother goddesses. They adopted "La Moreneta" who had a history of miracles.

10 PAPI LEFT

1950

I don't remember when Papi left. My parents met and married in New York City, where I was born. They were a very handsome couple. Mom was petite with clear pale skin and a small pointy nose, and brown hair and eyes. Papi was six feet tall with an olive complexion and black hair and eyes. He had a long pointy nose. People often asked if they were brother and sister. My father loved the ladies, but he kept Mom locked up in the house when he wasn't there. He liked to drink with his friends after work, and he came home with lipstick on his collar and on his shorts. This enraged Mami and they had terrible screaming battles. I loved my father, but Mami told me that I gave him my back after one of their screaming battles. Mami left him when I was 2 years old. She took me to Puerto Rico to my grandfather's house in Mayaguez. Mami wanted to divorce Papi, but Grandpa wouldn't hear it.

"A woman's place is with her husband," he told her.

"He was afraid I wanted to be a puta and go to bed with a lot of men," Mami said.

In the 1950s women didn't divorce their husbands. We returned to New York and Papi. Mami became pregnant and bore my sister, Peggy. I was 3 years old when Mami left him again. This time Grandpa saw the knife he left in her suitcase and he understood. Mami told us the story of the knife a few years later.

She walked into the kitchen and opened the silverware drawer. She pulled out a butter knife sharpened to a point. "He sharpened this knife in front of me every night. He said 'if you leave me, I will slash your face with it. No one will want you with your pretty face cut.' He came home with lipstick on his shorts again and we fought. I said I was going to leave him, and he pulled out this knife. He chased me down Broadway and 52nd Street with it. He tried to catch me, but I hid and stayed with a neighbor. The next day when he went to work, I got both of you from a neighbor and left for Puerto Rico. When I opened my suitcase in Puerto Rico, I found all my clothes slashed. He left the knife at the bottom of the suitcase. When Grandpa saw what he did, he shook his head. The next day, he drove me to the lawyer's office."

1955

I remember when Papi came to visit us five years after the divorce. I was eight years old and my sister was six. We lived in the South Bronx. This is where we moved when Mami remarried. That marriage didn't work out because he was having an affair with a married woman. Mom threw him out after he slapped her. We lived in an old railroad apartment where one room flowed into the other. Someone knocked on the metal front door. Mom answered the door and escorted a tall, dark, and handsome man and a tall, thin, smiling man into the living room. One sat on the green floral armchair and the other on our green floral couch.

"Girls, this is your father," Mami announced, pointing to the handsome man on the couch. Papi beamed at us. It was hard to resist his smile with those beautiful even white teeth. We smiled back. Mami was standing observing us with a stiff stern face like when she was angry and ready to hit us with the belt. We knew the other man. He was uncle Israel. He visited us a couple of times when we lived in Manhattan. He was tall and thin like my father, but not as handsome. He had a space in his front teeth like mine. He was a merchant marine and brought us presents from India when he visited us. He gave me a beautiful Indian Sarasvati goddess doll with long black hair and a red sari. She had four arms which I didn't understand, but I still liked the doll. He also gave us umbrellas made of bamboo rods and thick colorful paper. It had a very strong smell that I didn't recognize. Uncle was very kind. During his first visit, he stared at me long and hard. He said he wanted me to meet someone. He returned a couple of weeks later with his daughter. I looked at her and it was like looking into the mirror. I looked like her. She had a space in her front teeth and her hair and eyes were black like mine. Her skin was a dark olive. I was a couple of years younger and my skin was a lighter olive color like my father's, but I looked like her.

Now I smiled at uncle Israel, recalling his visits. He smiled and gave me a warm hug. Papi smiled at us. He had a handsome perfil, profile. He wore a light gray suit, a white shirt, a gray tie, and a black fedora. He said, "I am in New York for a couple of weeks and I wanted to see you". I sat next to him looking up at him. I missed him so much. I wanted to ask the question burning a hole in my heart, but I was hesitant. Finally, when there was a lull in the conversation, I blurted it out.

"Are you going to live with us now?"

He shot a half-smile at Mami. Her two eyes twitched at once and she didn't smile. She leaped from her chair and into the kitchen to prepare coffee. I didn't bring it up again.

He visited us again the following weekend. He stayed for a while and had coffee. Then he said, "I have to go."

"Oh, don't go. Where are you going?" I asked.

"I am going to the movies."

"To the movies! Oh, can we go? We never go to the movies."

He was hesitant but after a short while he said, "Okay, but we have to leave right now because I am picking up a friend." I was so excited. He drove to his friend's house in his brand new red and white De Soto sedan. His friend, Evelyn was a very young, attractive brunette. At her apartment, we met a lot of smiling pleasant people.

"Finally, we get to see your daughters," one of them said to Papi.

"We are family, primos, cousins," another smiling man said to me.

"How is your mother? We haven't seen her in years."

Before I could answer, Papi hustled us out the door with his friend.

"Vamos tarde para el cine, we are running late for the movies," Papi told them.

We arrived at the movies to a packed theater. Papi trolled around the theater and found two seats. He called me and my sister and sat us down. Then he and his friend walked to the front of the theater where they sat in two vacant seats. They talked for a while, and they weren't watching the movie. My sister and I sat watching them. Then they started necking. They looked like they were going to eat each other's faces off!

My sister and I looked at each other and closed our eyes.

"Eeyoo," Peggy said.

I was angry that he left us to be with her.

***

Nine months later, Papi called from Chicago. "Sorpresa, es Papi. You have a new sister. I called her Elaine." I didn't say anything, but I didn't like it. I called Mami over to the phone. "Mami, Papi is on the phone. He says I have a new sister. He called her Elaine like me." Mami's face twisted in a grimace as she grabbed the phone.

"You son of a bitch. How dare you call here to tell your daughter you have a baby. You don't support the children you have…you son of a bitch. Don't you ever call here again." She slammed the phone on the receiver. The bell inside the black table phone kept dinging long after she hung up. "That son of a bitch. That baby belongs to his cousin. She is 17 years old. He knocked her up the last time he was here. What he didn't tell us is that he already had a wife and a son in Chicago. All he cares about is nice clothes, new cars, and Florsheim shoes. He never thinks about sending you a card for your birthday or a present for Christmas. Nothing, nada. And you want me to take him back? I am taking that son of a bitch to court for child support. He hasn't given me a cent for you since the divorce. Now he will pay. I know where he lives."

I shifted about the room because I was the one who asked for his address so I could write to him.

Family Court

Mami took me with her to family court in Manhattan. I was sitting in the back row with her when Papi walked into the courtroom. He smiled at me. I smiled back. My mother, ignored him putting her little nose up in the air. The judge called Mami to the front of the courtroom. Smiling, Papi walked over and sat down next to me. Mami glared at us from the front of the courtroom. I looked down. I was afraid of her rage. The judge called Papi to the front. Later Mami was all smiles.

The judge ordered him to pay child support, and to buy beds for us. He paid the $15 child support for six months, and new bunk beds arrived at our apartment in the South Bronx. It was great to get a new bed. My other bed was a lumpy old cot.

One night while we were sleeping, two burly white men in black suits banged on our metal front door waking us up. Mami looked through the peephole to see who it was. They showed her identification. She opened the door.

"We are from the ABC collection agency," said, one man. The other wore a holstered gun, which he exposed as he opened his jacket and put his hand on his hip.

"We want to speak with Mr. Soto."

"He doesn't live here."

"Did you receive new bunk beds?"

"Yes, my ex-husband bought them for the girls."

"Well Mr. Soto put a down payment on the beds, but he didn't finish paying for them. We are here to collect the $86 balance."

"He doesn't live here. The court said he had to buy the beds for the girls. I can give you his address. He lives in Chicago."

"You have the beds so you have to pay or we will take you to jail." Our jaws dropped when he said that and tears rolled down our cheeks.

"Or we can take this Admiral television as payment." They bent down, grabbing the bottom of the console television.

"No, wait a minute," Mami said as she rushed out the door. She was gone for a while and we didn't know where she went. The men were looking at their watches and shifting around in their chairs.

She returned with the $86 and counted it out into the man's hand. My sister and I hugged each other in happiness. They weren't taking Mami to jail! Mami borrowed the money from Jenny, whose husband owned a Bodega in the neighborhood. The man pocketed the money. They left, but I never forgot.

Even so, I still missed my father.

***

One day Mami was yelling at Peggy.

"Sister Miriam called to tell me you missed school today after lunch."

"I went looking in the burned building across the street," said Peggy, whose face was black with soot. "Look, I found this Brownie camera in the coal near the furnace."

"You know I don't want you playing in those buildings you could get hurt in there. The buildings are burnt out and something could break and fall on you. Worse yet, one of the drunks that hang out in those buildings could grab you and hurt you."

"Nothing happened to me," Peggy said, walking away defiantly. "I wish Papi was here."

"That son of a bitch left because he doesn't care about you. All he cares about is putas, wearing nice clothes, new cars, and Florsheim shoes," Mami ranted. "You are so stupid. Do you think he cares about you? He doesn't even send the stinking $15 a month for child support. He never sends you a birthday card or a gift for Christmas. If you think he is so great, I will send you and your sister to live with him in Chicago. Then you will know what is good. He is a bastard, but if you miss him so much and want him, I will send you both to live with him."

My mother's words felt like daggers in my heart. I always pleased her, and I felt betrayed by her. She was going to punish me even though I was good in school, and I didn't mention that I missed my father. Peggy ran away from my mother's slaps. She hid behind the armchair, and under the bed when my mother chased her with the leather belt. I hid within myself. I didn't speak back or say that I missed my father. On that occasion, I became very hot. I laid on the cold floor in my bedroom to cool off. I had a fantasy that my mother was walking across the street and got hit by a car. She lay there dead with her legs splayed apart. I was happy for a moment, but then I felt fear. If she died, then we wouldn't have anyone to take care of us. I prayed to God that it wouldn't happen.

I didn't see my father again until I was 24 years old.

Sarasvati

11 ZARAGOZA, SPAIN

After our visit to Montserrat, we stayed at a seaside resort in the South of Spain near Almeria. I got up early to do yoga and meditate. During my meditation, I saw the image of a Church with twin spires. Before breakfast, I pulled out my travel book and saw the same church. The Church was in Zaragoza. It was a premier Marian sanctuary with a miraculous Black Madonna.

At breakfast, I spoke to my husband. "Nan, I know this is going to sound crazy, but I saw a Church with twin spires in my meditation today. Then, I was looking in my travel book and I found a picture of the same Church with twin spires. It is in Zaragoza. There is a miraculous Black Madonna there. I would love to go." I showed him the map and pointed to the location.

"Elaine, we have flight plans to Malaga and hotel reservations there. This Church is in the opposite direction of where we plan to go. We already paid for the hotel. We will lose our money for our flight and the hotel. On top of that, we will be paying for a new hotel that is if we can find one."

"I know it sounds crazy, but I want to go. I looked it up in Ean Begg's book and it says that the Madonna appeared to St. James there."

"Elaine, this is crazy. We are going to lose a lot of money and pay extra for hotels."

"Can you think about it?"

A couple of days later, while I was cooking dinner, I brought it up again.

"Nan, I still want to go to Zaragoza."

"Elaine, I don't want to do that. We already have everything set for Malaga."

"I know, but I only agreed to Malaga because our friends wanted to go there. It's not fair that we have to get stuck with their plan after they canceled on us. You know my main goal in traveling to Spain is to visit the Black Madonna. This one came to me. I already did a week in the South of Spain. It is nice, but I don't want to spend another week on the beach. I want to look for more Black Madonnas. OWWWWWW, I burned my hand." I pulled my hand away from the hot electric coil of the stovetop. Nan came over and looked at my hand. He looked in the refrigerator for something to soothe the burning. I put some butter on it. Quiet now, we sat down to dinner, but we were still riled up. My hand turned crimson and swelled. We went to the Red Cross Medical Care Unit in the Plaza. There we met two young Resident Doctors who were covering emergencies.

"How did you burn your hand?" the male Resident asked.

"I was stir-frying some vegetables on the stove. I got distracted because we were talking about going to Zaragoza."

"Zaragoza, I love Zaragoza," the pretty blond Resident said. "The Madonna appeared there many years ago. She left a pillar that people go to touch. They covered it in gold. There is a hole in the gold where you can touch it."

"I want to go there, but my husband doesn't want to change our travel plans."

"Oh, it is worth a change of plans," she said.

Nan listened as we talked and they bandaged my hand.

"There is a travel agency called Brujulas. They can help you make hotel arrangements. They have nice cheap hotels," she said.

Nan and I walked into the plaza. It was now dark and the park looked enchanted. The lights went on lighting up our path as we approached. We didn't speak until we returned to the hotel.

"You really want to change our plans?" Nan asked, looking away into the distance.

"I know it sounds crazy to you, but I do." I was afraid of his anger and disapproval like that of my mother. Dealing with his anger wasn't my strong suit, but I stood firm this time. I learned to survive as a child by avoiding Mom's anger, but the call to do this was strong.

"OK, we will call tomorrow and cancel the hotel and reschedule our flight."

"Yeah!" I said, jumping up and down hugging Nan.

We were able to cancel our hotel reservations in Malaga without penalty. I agreed to pay the flight cancellation fee and we rearranged our flight plan. We booked a very nice cheap hotel on the Plaza of the Basilica in Zaragoza. The sky was clear and blue and we passed fields of sunflowers along the countryside as we drove there. I took dozens of pictures of the luminous sunflowers. I never saw so many in one place at one time.

We arrived at the Plaza in Zaragoza. There we found a Basilica dedicated to La Virgen del Pilar. It had the two long spires that I saw in my meditation. The

Basilica was enormous. It took up half of the plaza. The front entrance was the original Church built by Santiago. They extended the old Church into the new Basilica like what they did at Montserrat. There was a huge altar with a porcelain sculpture of the Madonna surrounded by clouds and angels. She held a pillar in her outstretched hand, a depiction of the miracle of her apparition to Santiago. To the right of the main altar, there was a small one-foot statue of the Black Madonna carved in mahogany. According to Ean Begg, the Madonna gave the jasper pillar to Santiago. She asked him to build a chapel where she appeared to him near the Ebro River. The legend is that St. Luke, one of the Apostles sculpted the statue. The statue is very small in size and is Romanesque in style. The Black Madonna holds a child in her arms. The child holds a small blackbird in his palm. The small statue sits on a gold enclosed jasper column.

During World War II, the Cathedral was bombed. They left a rocket in the rafters as a reminder that it was a miracle that the Church survived. In the miracle of Colandia, a man lost his leg and it grew back with her intercession. In the rear of the altar, there is a single wooden pew. One can kneel and touch the jasper column through an opening in the gold enclosure. The jasper column is concave from the touch of the faithful who caress it in prayer. I knelt and prayed and touched the jasper column as I observed others doing. Her feast is on October 12. That was my mother's birthday.

Del Pilar

Valvanera

Logroño, Spain

This monastery is in the Rioja wine country. It is also known as the Valley of Venus. I looked out the window at the lush green valley as Nan drove up the single-lane road to the mountain top. He stopped several times to allow other drivers to pass along the narrow one-lane road. It was scary being so close to the edge of this high mountain road as we passed other vehicles. At the top of the mountain, we found the monastery enclosed within high walls. We parked and walked to the Church. It is a small church and there was no one there. There was an altar carved out of a tree stump with a lovely Madonna and Child enthroned in the center of the church.

The Madonna was not black.

She and the child are blond and their skin is polychrome white. Nan and I looked at each other disappointed. After driving up a perilous road to get here, there was no Black Madonna. In his Gazetteer, Ean Begg wrote that there was a Black Madonna here. We sat and prayed and walked around the small quiet chapel.

Then I noticed a stained glass window behind the main altar. The colors were brilliant cobalt blue and red. The image is of a brown-skinned Madonna and a child sitting in a tree. She wears a crown in the shape of a beehive. White manna floats from her hand.

This was the Black Madonna Ean Begg wrote about. After praying to the Madonna, we went to the monastery looking for the hotel entrance. Walking along the hallway we passed a monk sitting at a long table counting small stacks of money. He focused on his task, noting the amounts in a ledger. He didn't look up or seem to notice us. As we passed him, a heavyset monk in a brown hooded habit hurried to us.

"Hello, can I help you," he asked.

"Yes, we are looking for a room for the night." The monk smiled. With a gallant gesture of his outstretched right arm, he pointed to the registration desk.

"How long would you like to stay?"

"One night, please. Do you have a restaurant?" Nan asked.

"Yes, it is where everyone eats. The food is delicious." The monk smiled, rubbing his rotund stomach. "Dinner is at 6 pm."

We washed up in our well-appointed room and walked around the monastery grounds. From the vantage point of the monastery, the mountains formed a V shape all the way down to the valley below. It was a luscious green place. We climbed to the top of the hill. I read that there was an old shrine to Venus, the Goddess of love here. We didn't see it because there was a tall metal chain link fence closing off the area.

My Journey to the Black Madonna

La Valvanera

    Winding one lane lush green mountain road
    Valley of Venus-La Valvanera
    Cabernet Sauvignon, Merlot
    Wines of Spain in the Monastery

    Valley of Venus-La Valvanera
    Searching for the Black Madonna
    Wines of Spain in the Monastery
    The Madonna was blond

    Searching for Black Madonnas
    Empty Church
    The Madonna was blond
    Sitting in the tree stump

    Empty Church
    Red wine at dinner amazing
    Sitting in a tree stump
    Behind her the black one glowed

Elaine Soto

Red wine at dinner amazing
Winding one lane lush green mountain road
Behind her the black one glowed
Cabernet Sauvignon, Merlot

La Valvanera

12 SPAIN

1999

On our second trip to Montserrat, Nan and I arrived at the Basilica at 6:30 pm. To our delight, we heard the angelic voices of L'Escalonia, the all-boys choir singing in the Church. The Hotel de la Abadia de Montserrat has changed since our last visit. It was no longer like monks' quarters, although they still had the same single metal beds in the rooms. The floors were now a combination of wood and rugs. The headboards now had carvings with the image of the Madonna of Montserrat. In the window, they installed window boxes with red geraniums. It was a hazy warm day, but cooler than the day before. It was a welcome change to arrive at the monastery. The stress in Malaga at the airport tired us out and threw a wrench in our travel plans. The airplane pilots were on strike and many flights were delayed and others canceled.

At the Malaga airport, we waited for four hours. We watched as our connecting flight to Barcelona went from delayed to canceled. I located our luggage while Nan rented a car. I was waiting for the elevator with my luggage when a traveler asked where I picked up my luggage. I stepped away from my cart to point the way. When I turned around, I saw a handsome tanned man pushing my cart into the elevator. I pulled the cart away from him. The handsome tanned man smiled a wry smile and boarded the elevator without looking back. I took the next elevator to ground level where I found Nan waiting in line to rent a car. I told him what happened with the luggage and he gave me a hug, "It's a good thing you noticed!"

We rented a Renault diesel engine car and drove to Barcelona. We stopped driving before dark and picked the closest hotel to the main road. There we slept in a bed that was too soft and too lumpy. The area was very noisy. There were bikers shooting off firecrackers in the middle of the night. Not a good night's sleep. I woke up itchy and scratching myself. We looked but we didn't find bed bugs.

While at Montserrat, we visited the gift shop. I was chatting with the clerk. I mentioned that Monserrate is my Confirmation name. She told me that I could get a special certificate with my name signed by the priest. She directed me to the Church office. When I arrived another clerk asked me to sign a guest register with my name and address. The priest looked at the guest register. He gave me a picture of the Black Madonna. He also gave me a certificate with my Confirmation name, Monserrate in calligraphy.

I was very touched by the gesture.

La Sagrada Familia

Barcelona

We visited the Church created by the Catalan architect, Antoni Gaudi. Gaudi was the greatest exponent of Catalan Modernism. Most of his works have a one-of-a-kind style. La Sagrada Familia was like climbing a mountain. The steps were steep. At each landing, there were small portals to view the art treasures inside the building. I was short of breath after our climb to the top. When we left the Church a small group of thieves accosted us. First, a thin tan-skinned woman stepped in front of us holding her stomach like she was in pain. She raised her hand to her mouth as if to say she was hungry. While we were looking at her, a small group of men surrounded us. In my peripheral vision, I saw a man opening the top zipper of Nan's backpack. Nan felt it and turned around. He pulled me to his side away from the group. He became very angry and told them to back off. Then he grabbed my arm and we crossed the street. We were walking through the middle of a small park to get to our car when Nan stopped and looked back. Two men were following us. There was an older man at the edge of the park directing them with hand gestures. Nan and I stopped and decided to double back and walk around the park. They lost sight of us. When we were driving out of the parking garage, we saw them again looking around puzzled.

Montjuich

We visited Montjuich, a Museum in Barcelona that houses ancient Black Madonnas. There were some in the Roman and Gothic sections of the Museum. The Roman Madonnas were 12th & 13th Century wooden statues. There was also an installation of parts of a fresco. It depicted Mary Magdalene as an apostle with hands lifted, leading a group in prayer. The image resembled the mosaic on the stairs to the Black Madonna's chapel at Montserrat. There was also a mural of a group of crowned women seated at a table like the apostles at the last supper. They raised their hands aloft giving a blessing.

In the Gothic section, there was a painting of St. Peter as Pope. Two angels accompanied him wearing white tunics. The tunics had red crisscrosses on them. The pope's robe had images of Mary Magdalene, along the border. They depict her as a priestess and pope. She holds a grail cup. This was the work of an Italian Renaissance painter.

Cadiz

I sat at the edge of the Mediterranean Sea meditating. We were staying at the Dona Lola Resort in Malaga. I saw the image of an angel wearing an antique helmet. He pointed behind me in the direction of Cadiz. Then in a flash of light, I saw the Black Madonna. I looked up what Churches or Sanctuaries were in the East in my travel book. I found the Santuario of La Virgen de la Regla in Chipiona. Nan was reluctant to travel there because it was two hours away from where we were staying. He finally agreed when I shared my meditation experience with him. The next morning, we drove two hours to Chipiona, Cadiz to visit La Virgen de la Regla.

We arrived at noon and found the Franciscan Sanctuary closed. There was a sign outside saying it was open until 1 pm and the guidebook said it was open until 1 pm. There was now a sign saying it would reopen at 5 pm. Nan got cranky. So did I. He wanted to go back to the Dona Lola Resort. We experienced this frustration several times on this journey. I showed him the travel guide. He thought I didn't check the time. This time I was sure I had the right time. We decided to wait four hours until the Sanctuary reopened. We had already driven two hours to get there. There was a quiet café nearby and we stopped there to have lunch. After lunch, we walked along the peaceful southern Andalusian waterfront. It was a very quiet town devoid of all the tourists we encountered in the Moorish white towns of Malaga. While we waited, I took pictures. A friendly resident saw us and asked if we wanted our picture taken. We agreed and we have a nice recuerdo of our visit standing in front of the Andalusian waterfront.

The priest opened the Sanctuary at 5 pm. We were the only people there. We prayed to a lovely statue of La Virgen de la Regla. She is black and holds a white baby. It is the first time I saw the Black Virgin holding a white baby. I took pictures of the Madonna holding a white child. After a while, the priest walked over to us and engaged us in conversation. I told him that I was a painter and I was researching the Black Madonna. He took us into the sacristy and he let us climb up a mahogany staircase to the back of the altar. The Madonna was high up on the altar. I photographed the Madonna from there. He mentioned that a small donation would help the Church. We gave him a donation. He invited us to see something special. He took us outside to the atrium. It was El Patio de la Plata. It sported walls, and benches covered with antique gothic blue and white tiles. It was a special treat to see.

St. Augustin commissioned La Bella Africana, La Virgen Libica. Monks hid it during the Muslim invasion in the 8th century. It remained hidden in a cistern near a fig tree until 1330. A monk received a vision and found the statue in what is now called El Humilladero near the Church. There is a history of miracles for this Black Madonna. There is a procession on her Feast Day, September 8th. This is

Mary's birthday. Earlier history reports that the Santuario sits over a castle-like temple. African hermits inhabited it during the 5th Century.

I painted this Madonna when we moved to Florissant, Colorado in 2001. I painted it in encaustic. I collaged some black crochet yarn for her hair and rice paper for the background. Nan and I built a ranch-style house on top of a mountain 9500 feet above sea level. We designed it together with a computer program. It included a large painting studio for me. Our property had ponderosa pines twisted into various unusual shapes. Native Americans marked their vison quests. They twisted saplings in the direction they were traveling. The saplings grew and kept the unusual shapes. Many of the trees were over 100 years old. Our house was on top of the mountain and faced Crystal Peak. That was the destination for the vision quests.

While we were building our house, a deer visited us. She hid from the afternoon sun under our long porch. I left apples for her and she ate them. She disappeared for a while. Then one morning she returned with two precious does. It was a treat for this New York City gal to see them up close and personal. There were also foxes in a den under a huge boulder across from our road. Nan and I saw the little foxes playing on top of the boulder one afternoon when we were taking a walk. Bears visited and opened our garbage cans looking for food, and cougars screamed at night. Those were both scary. I enjoyed hiking with my Keeshond, Bella. We climbed up to tree line or 10,000 feet on Pikes Peak. We both got tired there and returned. Pikes Peak is 14,000 feet above sea level. The winters were very cold in Florissant like in Peekskill and the snow was as abundant. This made it difficult and dangerous to drive to work. I had a psychotherapy office an hour away in Colorado Springs. We lived in Florissant for three years. Nan got a new job and we left for the warmer climate and culture of Albuquerque, New Mexico.

Elaine Soto

Virgen de la Regla

13 ITALY

1997

I took my first trip to Italy with Christians in the Visual Arts. We were studying the narrative church murals of the Renaissance. They tell the life of Christ. Not everyone had access to the bible or was able to read. Besides studying this I was also on my quest to find the Black Madonna of Italy. Ean Begg documented five Black Madonna sites in the Cult of the Black Virgin. I visited two of these on this trip.

The group arrived in Rome, and a van drove us to Orvieto. We visited el Duomo, a Cathedral with a gothic façade of gold, black and white mosaic. As part of our study of the Art of the Renaissance, we saw the frescos of Luca Signorelli in the Cathedral. We also visited el Pozo de San Patricio, an ancient well with a circular staircase. The next morning, we drove two hours to Assisi. There were lovely views of rolling hills and hilltop towns. My sensitive stomach was very queasy from the drive. I don't do well on very curvy roads.

At the Basilica of St. Francis, we saw the earliest murals of Giotto. They depict the life story of St. Francis and his miracles. He lived between 1181 and 1226. Each painting depicts a scene from the story of his life. The paintings cohere as a sequence, but they don't make sense if you don't know the background story. The theme that runs through the paintings is his experience of the miraculous. He like the Gnostics relied on internal knowing and personal experience. As I knelt praying in the Church, I felt the quiet calm presence of St. Francis. It felt like cool water running over a mountain stream. His presence filled the chapel. I felt quiet and at peace there.

I felt an urge to visit the Church of St. Claire a mile away. I walked over to the Church. Assisi is a beautiful quaint little town with small shops. There was no one in the Church when I arrived. A statue of St. Claire lay on top of her tomb. She dressed in a nun's habit. She was a follower of St. Francis and she founded a female monastic order. She was the first woman to write the rules of an order. I stared at her image amazed. St. Claire was a black woman. This was very different from the images I saw of her in Catholic School holy cards and paintings. St. Claire was my sister's Confirmation saint and in all the images I ever saw of her she was lily-white.

The two Black Madonnas I found on this trip were in Padova and Venice. La Madonna Mora de

Puydarrieux is in the Church of St. Anthony. She is a beautiful dark woman who wears a golden crown and holds a scepter in her hand. The legend is that Saint Anthony bought the statue in France and brought it to Padova. He was a devotee of the Black Madonna and the statue was at first placed in the Church above his coffin. It is now in its own chapel on the left side of the Church. I visited this Church at the end of my trip with the Christians in Visual Arts. I went alone to visit this Black Madonna. I found it in Ean Begg's Gazetteer. I was feeling sad about my impending separation from my fellow artists as I walked alone to the Church. In the Church, I knelt before the beautiful Black Madonna and I cried. The sadness gave way to a feeling of peace. Visiting the Black Madonna affirms me and my feelings. I love seeing a woman of color who has power and is equal to a man. My motivation for finding the Black Madonna was born of rejection as a woman of color. It made me go out and search for the positive hidden in a miracle-working Black Madonna.

The second Black Madonna I saw was in Venice. Our van dropped us off at the Piazza di San Marco. I left the group and walked along the small bridges crossing over the canals. I walked to the Basilica of Santa Maria Della Salute. On my way, I heard an oarsman on a gondola singing "O sole Mio" to a group of tourists on his boat. The acoustics on the water carried the sound loud and clear. It was divine. I promised myself to return with Nan one day so we could experience this magical place together. When I arrived at the basilica of Santa Maria de Salute, there was no one inside. There was a Byzantine Icon of the Mother of Health. It was from Crete and painted in the 13th Century. The Black Madonna was La Mesopanditissa, the Mesopotamian. According to their legend, St. Luke, the apostle painted it. I asked the church custodian if they had images of the Madonna that I could buy. He showed me all the religious articles with images of the Madonna stored in a glass display case. Noting my interest and my purchases, he gave me a gold-plated medal of La Mesopanditissa as a gift.

I painted her image in encaustic when I returned to my studio at Taller Boricua.

La Mesopanditissa

Manfredonia, Italy

On my second trip to Italy, my husband and I drove 2000 miles. We drove along the Adriatic Sea looking for Black Madonna sites. We were staying at a timeshare in Vieste. On our way to Vieste, we often asked for travel directions at toll booths. Several times they gave us directions to San Giovanni Rotondo. They assumed we wanted to visit the Church of Padre Pio. We stayed in Vieste overnight. In the morning we drove to Manfredonia in search of the Black Madonna called La Sipontina. When we arrived at the Church we found it closed. Since we had time before the Church reopened, we decided to visit the Church of Padre Pio. This was the Church they sent us to visit every time we asked for direction. I heard about Padre Pio from Nan's mother years before. He was an Italian friar, priest, stigmatist, mystic, and now a saint in the Catholic Church. Nan's mother, Angela told us that her friend attended a mass that he gave many years ago. She said that when Padre Pio gave her friend communion a drop of blood from his palm fell on her white blouse. He had the stigmata of Christ on his hands and feet like St. Francis. She showed Angela the blouse. When I researched Padre Pio on the Internet, I found some information about him. Seeing statues of him on several sites, I began to think he was dead. In the Church, I learned he died in 1968.

From there, we drove to Mont Sant Michel in the Gargano Mountains. I read in Ean Begg's book that there was a Black Madonna there. The legend is that Michael the Archangel appeared to a man in a cave. The Church is at the top of a mountain in the cave. Inside, many people were kneeling in prayer before a small altar. There was no Black Madonna visible. There was an empty niche by the entrance to the cave where it may have been before. We visited the Church's museum, which held a few old relics of an earlier Church but no Black Madonna.

The next day we left Vieste earlier to visit La Sipontina in Manfredonia. Driving on the curvy road from the east coast of Italy to Foggia, I felt my stomach turn upside down.

"Honey, can you slow down. I am going to throw up."

Nan slowed down and pushing the lever on my seat down, he said, "lay back, you might feel better lying down." I did but I still wanted to puke. I tried to focus on the scenery. In a bend on the road, a red-faced man was selling olive oil in clear glass bottles with a cork stopper. He displayed his bottles on a folding table that was his roadside stand. He tended his olive trees on the hillside near his roadside stand. I made a mental note to come back and buy some olive oil from him when we returned. We came back late and I never saw him again.

We arrived at Manfredonia at 12:30 pm at a vacant parking lot and locked Church doors. "Ugh!" I said.

"I'll find out when they reopen the Church." Seeing a parking attendant in the lot, I asked, "Signore a cuale hora aperto la Chiesa?

"Aperto a la cinque, Signora," the slender hunched-over man replied.

"At five! What will we do here for four and a half hours?" Nan asked.

"We can go have lunch. It might settle my stomach. What do you think?"

"Okay," he said. In my best Italian, I asked the elderly gentleman for a good restaurant nearby.

"En el Porto." He pointed in the direction of the Gulf of Manfredonia and gestured with his hand for us to follow him. He pointed to a small white building with a sculpture of La Madonna Della Spiga, Madonna of the wheat sheaf. There was a white round fountain with a puti peeing into the basin next to a large sign for La Antica. Rubbing his stomach and smiling, he said, "Buon restaurante, il pesce fresco." He pointed to the wharf where fishermen were busy unloading their catch of the day.

Speaking a mixture of Italian and Spanish, we chatted with him for a while and learned about Il Castello. It was an old castle converted into an anthropological museum. He encouraged us to visit while we waited.

"Grazie, Signore."

"Prego."

We walked over to the marina and watched the fishermen loading the fresh fish from the boat into carts. They carried them to a large hangar-type building across the street. Men in aprons and big black gloves prepared the fish for the market. Outside we heard the loud sounds of the men talking, laughing, and chopping off fish heads. The saline smell of the sea and the fish filled the air. Il Castello was across the street from the wharf. After a tasty fish lunch, we walked over to the anthropological museum to see the exhibit. It was an exhibition of antique clay jugs attached to a reproduction of an old ship's galley.

"How did they stand those jars up. They come to a point at the bottom," I mused out loud.

"They put them on a metal stand and used them when they needed them," a handsome dark-skinned man said. He introduced himself as the archeologist who discovered the jars in an old sunken ship a few miles away. The Greeks, Africans, and Romans colonized this area. Ships often sank carrying cargo such as this. This may have been a ship from Africa. The Romans preferred to travel along the Appian Way. They conducted commerce and war through there. The bloodiest war occurred in Cannes. They colonized the people of the area. King Manfred, the son of Phillip II established this city. It retains his name."

We returned to the Cathedral of San Lorenzo at 5 pm when it opened for mass. There we saw a Byzantine icon of Mary called La Sipontina. It is facing the main entrance of the plaza as you walk into the Church. We walked to the front of the church to view it. On the right side of the main entrance in her own chapel is another beautiful Black Madonna. It is a wooden statue called La Madonna Degli Oggi Sibirati, Madonna of the Staring Eyes. She sits in a throne position with the Christ child on her lap. She has a very strong presence.

We also visited the old church outside of town where La Sipontina first resided. The crypt of the Church was very interesting in its gothic structure and eaves.

There was no history of miracles for this Madonna.

The Black Virgin in Lucera had a history of miracles. We drove two hours to Lucera but the Madonna was not on view. The church attendant said the statue was out for restoration. Disappointed, we drove on to Napoli.

Napoli

We arrived in the center of Naples at 2:30 pm. It was rush hour. An onslaught of cars greeted us driving in and out of the city. A traffic cop dressed in a beige uniform blew his whistle. He directed traffic with a white-gloved hand. I asked him for directions.

"Signore, dove la Chiesa di Santa María Maggiore?" He motioned for us to pull over to the side of the road.

"La Chiesa, vada dirito," he said, pointing ahead with his white-gloved hand. Looking at me he smiled and pointed to the camera hanging from my neck. In a mixture of Spanish and Italian, he told me to put it away. With his hand, he made a yanking gesture at his neck.

I said, "Someone can steal it?" he nodded. I hid the camera under my car seat. "Grazie, Signore."

"Prego, Prego," he said.

We drove on searching for the Church, but we couldn't find it. What we found was a traffic circle that sent us to the other side of town. I asked a short, slim Italian lady for directions in my best Italian. "Senora, dove la Chiesa di Santa Maria Maggiore?" The lady smiled, amused at my attempt to speak Italian.

"Bella," she said, holding my chin and pointing to the left.

We drove to the left and found ourselves on a side street jammed with traffic. Cars and Vespa scooters tried to pass double-parked cars and a truck making.

It was a narrow side street. We were all stuck there. A man got out of his car and directed traffic getting everyone past the truck. We had a hair's breadth of space to pass.

"Grazie signore," we all said to him as we squeezed past the double-parked truck.

"Prego, Prego," he said to each of us.

When we got to the corner, there was a light. A stream of Vespa scooters whizzed past cars, trucks, and pedestrians. They knew how to get around this city.

Lost again we stopped a lady dressed in black walking with a younger woman. I asked for directions to the Basilica. She didn't understand Italian, so I spoke to her in Spanish. She couldn't answer. She said she was Brazilian and spoke Portuguese in broken Italian and Spanish. In the universal language of pointing and hand signals, she offered to take us there. She and her daughter got in the car and pointed the way until we arrived at the Church. We offered to drive her home, but she refused, thanked us, and walked away.

Carmine Maggiore

Inside the Basilica of Carmine Maggiore, there is an icon of Santa Maria di Maggiore. The Church is large, but the structure is narrow and long. The walls in the back of the Church behind the Black Madonna had a lot of retablos. They depicted the Black Madonna healing people who were bedridden. There were also Milagros under glass attesting to the miracles of the Madonna. I photographed everything. We scurried out of the Church because our luggage was visible in the car and we didn't want to tempt thieves. We tried to find the hotel where we were staying overnight, but we got lost. There was construction near the hotel. We drove around in circles several times before we gave up in frustration and left for Rome.

14 FRANCE

1998

I met Lorna Roberts at a lecture she gave on the Black Madonna at the New York Open Center. She announced a tour to the Black Madonna sites of France. She was a shaman. I wanted to search for the Black Madonna in France, but I didn't speak French. This tour was perfect for my journey and I signed up. Selling Black Madonna paintings gave me the money to do this.

On the airplane to Paris, I took a short nap and woke up with a jolt. I saw a beautiful Madonna dressed in white seated on a throne. She held a white rosary and a white dove hovered over her head. We arrived at Charles De Gaulle airport. The group stopped for a snack before we rode for two hours in a Volkswagen van to Chartres. Some of the women spoke at length about a Shamanic Journey they took with Lorna

Roberts to Nazca Peru. They said it is a powerful place.

After breakfast, we visited Chartres Cathedral. The blue of the stained glass windows in the church is the most beautiful blue I have ever seen. The Madonna du Chartres and the Madonna of the Crypt were both brown wooden statues. They are very different from each other. Our Lady of the Pillar is six feet tall and stands on a pillar. Brown wooden hearts surrounded her. She wore a triangular pink gown and held the Christ child to her heart. There were a lot of people praying in front of her altar and the energy there was very strong. People seemed stuck in place taking pictures and beholding the Madonna. I felt the same attraction to the spot as I did at Montserrat in Spain. This Madonna could also be at a spot marking a wouvire or a ley line in the area. The Knights Templar positioned churches according to ancient power spots. They built windows in the church to allow views of the moon and some planets at certain times of the year. Later I joined a small group of people in the crypt of the Church to view a second Black Madonna, the Madonna of the Crypt. This wooden statue is brown and rustic. The Black Madonna wore a crown and sat enthroned with a child on her lap. The energy here was very quiet and grounding. There was an old well used by the Druids for healing ceremonies. It was now covered with a wooden board.

In a store across from the Cathedral on the South transept, I picked up a couple of small unicorn tapestries. One tapestry was of a lady in a garden and one of a unicorn. They are both symbolic of the hidden story of Jesus and Mary Magdalene. Mary is the Lady left behind in the garden. Jesus is the miraculous unicorn corralled by society and separated from his consort.

Chartres Cathedral
>
> Cobalt blue stained glass
>
> A blue never before beheld
>
> Madonna du Chartres
>
> Brown wooden hearts surround
>
>
>
> A blue never before beheld
>
> Queen of hearts
>
> Brown wooden hearts surround
>
> Atop a pillar the Queen is brown
>
>
>
> Queen of hearts
>
> In attendance
>
> Atop a pillar the Queen is brown
>
> Awed we stood
>
>
>
> In attendance
>
> Another in the crypt enthroned
>
> Awed we stood
>
> Druid portal in a well

Elaine Soto

Another in the crypt enthroned
Cobalt blue stained glass
Druid portal in a well
Madonna du Chartres

Riom and Geneste

From the Cathedral, we rode in a van to Riom, Geneste, and Clermont Ferrand. It was a five-hour ride, and it drizzled all the way there and became colder. I went into a sound sleep for a couple of hours, and I meditated and prayed. While in meditation, I saw a tunnel extending beyond the back of our van. A narrow brick stairwell descended into the tunnel, a path into the earth. Then I saw a beautiful Black Madonna sitting on a throne wearing a gold crown. Her dress was cadmium red and she wore a turquoise blue cloak draped over her shoulders. She looked like our lady of Montserrat. The colors were vivid. She was serene and very peaceful.

In Geneste the Black Madonna was in the dark in a chapel on the right-hand side of the Church. We lit candles to see her better and to take pictures. In the following picture, I am holding a candle to reveal her image for the group.

In Riom, the Black Madonna was in a large room behind a crisscrossed metal gate. I photographed her through one of the small openings in the gate.

La Geneste

My Journey to the Black Madonna

Riom

Shamanic Journey

Our group stayed at Chateau de Roquetaillade. It is a medieval castle in Bordeaux in the South of France. There was an old observatory where the original owner watched and studied the stars. There was also an old Church dusty and in disrepair. We met in a section of the Church for our Shamanic Journey where we stood alongside dusty church pews. There was a lovely carved marble altar with an image of Mary Magdalene writing in a book carved on the side. Lorna smudged and cleared our energy with incense. We brought candles, flowers and whatever was meaningful for us to share. I brought a rattle and a small wooden statue of the Black Madonna of Montserrat. We burned candles, lit incense, chanted, and shook our rattles to get into a sacred space. We introduced ourselves and shared what we wanted to do on this journey. We talked for three hours. I shared my feelings of loss for my father and my anger with my mother. We wrote what we wanted to heal on a piece of paper. I burned mine in front of my Black Madonna and with it released my mother.

Lorna later took us to a lovely wooded area where we formed a circle and chanted. Some grounded their energy by laying down on the grass. Some cried and mourned their recent losses. Some of us received telepathic messages from loved ones now gone. I received a message for a woman who was lying on the grass crying. She lost her sister a few months earlier. She worried because she didn't know if her sister was okay. The message I received was from her sister saying "I'm okay. Do not worry about me." Her sister was very relieved to hear that message.

Lorna then took us to another wooded area nearby. She told us that they hung or burned women healers at the stake there. They accused them of witchcraft. Seventy-five to eighty percent of the witches were women. The Church also used charges of heresy and witchcraft against the Knights Templar. They waged a 150-year Inquisition against the Cathars in the 13th and 14th Centuries. The Knights Templar and the Cathars safeguarded many early Christian artifacts. Witchcraft was a pre-Christian religion. In 1484 the Church hierarchy said it interfered with the work of the Church. When we visited the site of the hangings and burnings, many of us felt a profound sadness. We prayed for the souls of those who lost their lives for their beliefs.

After the meeting, we drove to Marsat where we saw a beautiful Black Madonna (Verge Noir de Marsat). Lorna heard there was another Black Madonna in Thuret. We didn't have any information about the Church or know if it was open. The group agreed to take a chance detour to visit the church. It was in the center of the small town of Thuret. We were lucky because it was open. The Church dated from the Roman era, according to a plaque outside. Inside some of the town's people lit candles under a picture of Mary Magdalene. She reclined on the grass under a tree reading a book. There was a skull laying on the ground beside her. Some people in the church listened to a "canned" mass and prayed in the pews.

There was no priest and they played a tape recording of a priest saying mass over a loudspeaker. Behind the altar, there was a beautiful stained glass window. It had a heart and a cross. Outside the Church, there was a sign with a heart and in the center, there were small xxx's. These xxx's are a symbol of the Church of Amor and the Cathars. Inside the Church, there was a sarcophagus lying on the ground. There was the image of a knight carved into the marble cover of the sarcophagus. Inside the Church near the pulpit, there was a 3-foot-tall Black Madonna. Called Vierge Noire des Croisades. Her face was black and she wore a cape made of brown sackcloth. The Crusaders carried this Madonna with them for protection. The Crusaders were an army sent to France by Pope Innocent III to rout out the Cathars. To them, the Cathars were heretics because they accepted no creed, dogma, or canon. The Cathars who lived a pure life felt that they needed no intercessor to experience the divine. They taught that God did not punish. This took the power of atoning for original sin away from the Church. The Cathars believed that each person learns from experience and self-corrects. They believed in the equality of the sexes and that women receive enlightenment. They accepted women as priests.

St Marie de la Mer

We visited the statue of Saint Sara in the crypt of the Church of St. Marie de la Mer in the South of France. Worshippers covered the statue with layers of pink, blue, and purple tulle. The crypt was dark and the statue has a dark complexion with black hair and eyes, a straight nose, and thin lips. In the glow of the candlelight, her image is warm, strong, and appealing. People mill around the statue in the crypt to pray, light candles, and take pictures. They then proceed outside of the underground stillness. She is majestic, and she has a very old presence.

The gypsies who have a history of social rejection adopted Sara as their saint and call her Sara Kali. Sara means queen in Hebrew and Kali Ma is the Indian mother goddess of transformation. In 1686, they painted Sara's face black as a cult object. The Gypsies celebrate the selection of their new Queen in the crypt of this Church.

The French celebrate the feast of Mary Magdalene on June 24th. They carry the statue of St. Sara in a procession out to sea. We attended this procession when I visited. There were people dressed in medieval costumes. They wore velvet berets and ruffled dress shirts and red velvet jackets with gold piping. They rode white horses and carried banners to the shore. They released a small boat with the statue of St. Sara out to sea.

The legend of St. Sara is that she was an Egyptian servant. She accompanied the three Maries on their journey from Jerusalem to Marseilles. In reality, Sara was the daughter of Jesus and Mary Magdalene. They concealed her identity to protect her from the persecutors of the Christians. The three Maries were Mary Magdalene, Mary Salome, and Mary Jacobi.

The story at Saint Marie de la Mer in the South of France is that they set the three Maries adrift on the open sea. They were in a frail boat from Palestine without sails or oars. They arrived in Marseilles, where the King received them like royalty. Two of the Maries stayed in the area. According to the legend, Sara married into the French royal bloodline. Her offspring are the Merovingians. The Merovingian is the royal bloodline of Jesus and Mary Magdalene.

Mary Magdalene went on to live in a cave in St. Baume. It is a natural grotto dug by erosion and a power spot in the French Alps of Provence. She lived there for 30 years. She ministered to the people of France as Jesus requested of the apostles. They buried her at St. Maxim and built a church there in her honor.

St. Baume

We visited the cave at St Baume. When we walked in it was dark and cool inside. There were a couple of wall sconces with candles lighting the grotto. There was a mahogany pew on the left-hand side where my friend knelt, prayed, and cried. She was recently widowed. I prayed sitting on a wooden bench nearby. The floor was dirt. The grotto was quiet and peaceful. They closed it for renovation in 1997. A picture of it after the renovations showed a tiled floor, new wall sconces, and more pews.

At St. Baume, there were books and pamphlets about Mary Magdalene's life. This was the second time I heard that she was the Bride of Christ. The first time was in New York in 1997. I attended a panel presentation on the Black Madonna held at the New York Open Center. The presenters were Lorna Roberts, Diane Wolkstein, China Galland, and Suzi Gablik. They presented that the Merovingians were the descendants of Jesus and Mary Magdalene. Merovingian means mother of the vine or the Hebrew royal bloodline. The fleur de Lis is the royal emblem of the Merovingian kings.

In another story, a priest in Rennes de Chateau in France found hidden documents. They were under the altar of his Church. These documents disclosed the lineage of the Merovingian kings. He brought the documents to the Church hierarchy. They say the Church gave him a tidy sum to hide his discovery.

Educated in Catholic School it was hard for me to integrate this information. What I learned in Catholic School was that Jesus was celibate. I learned he never married. I learned that Mary Magdalene was a prostitute. I hesitated to share what I learned in France. I was afraid of rejection for being a heretic. In Catholic School, the nuns discouraged questioning. I heard about the Crusades as a positive way of spreading Christianity. I did not hear that they killed those who didn't agree with the Church's teachings. I knew that they excommunicated those who didn't follow the Church doctrine. In Catholic school, they said that divorced people were not considered part of the Church. They excommunicated them. I didn't tell anyone about my mother's divorce. When asked about my father, I said he was dead. I didn't want to get thrown out of Catholic school or get excommunicated.

Although I was afraid of being a heretic, I included the information I learned on my journey in France. I had a retrospective show at Union Theological Seminary titled the "Divine Feminine". I created a catalog for the exhibition. In it, I shared that Mary Magdalene is the Black Madonna in France. She is black because she represents something occult or hidden in the Church. The Church hides that Jesus and Mary Magdalene were married. When my mother read the catalog, she said she would not share it with her friends. She always shared my successes with her friends. She feared her friends would think I was "crazy".

Later, she shared that she and Tia Chencha dedicated me to the Black Madonna of Montserrat when I was a baby. Chencha was the black neighbor who watched over Mami when she was a young girl. She gave her coffee in the morning when her parents went to work. She loved her coffee.

I had no idea my mother and Tia Chencha dedicated me to the Black Madonna. It was a tremendous surprise. It helped me understand my strong unconscious attraction to the Black Madonna.

St. Sara

Le Puy en Veley

We arrived at Le Puy in Veley. The Basilica of Notre Dame du Puy sat in a promontory formed by a volcanic eruption a million years ago. The belief is that St. Louis IX, King of France gave the first Black Madonna to the church in 1254 AD. The first miracle occurred when the Virgin told a widow with a malignant fever to lie down on the fever stone. It healed her.

When I went to the Church I didn't know the story of the fever stone. But, when I walked past the black stone lying flat near the entryway, I was very attracted to it. I sat on it and it felt quiet and soothing. No one in the church noticed the stone. There was no documentation about the miracle.

Le Puy is a pilgrimage site for successful childbirth. It is also one of the four main starting points to El Camino de Santiago de Compostela in northern Spain.

When I returned home from France, I decided to paint a series of Black Madonnas from France. I was meditating on a mat in my studio at Taller Boricua when I saw the image of the Black Madonna of Le Puy en Veley. In the meditation, I saw myself as a three-year-old child talking to my father as I did before he left us. My mother always said he left us and I believed that, but the truth is my mother left him. She filed for divorce. The Black Madonna of Le Puy was holding me as a child and without words said "I love you as you are". It is hard when you are a child and your parents separate and divorce. I felt it was my fault. I wasn't good enough. Painting this Black Madonna was healing for me.

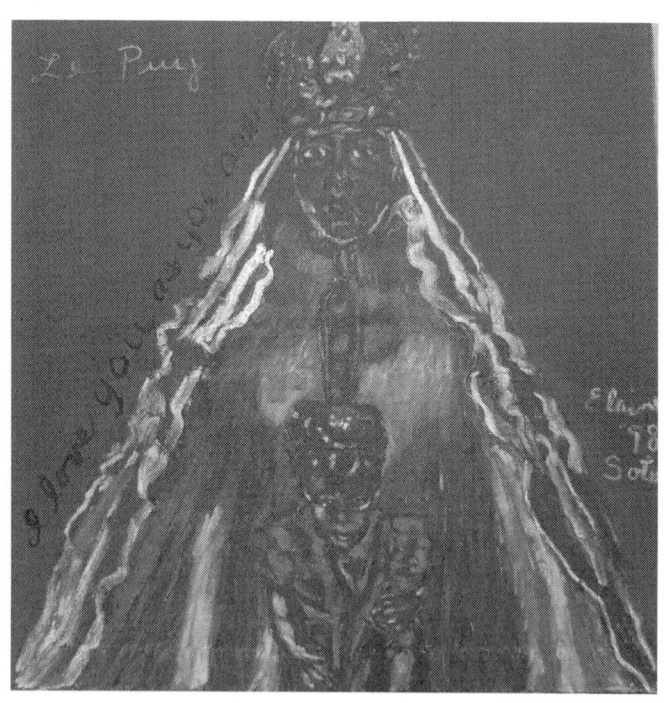

Le Puy

My Journey to the Black Madonna

I love you as you are
        Le Puy en Veley
        Beautiful Black Madonna of France
        I saw you
        Famous for the miracle of the fever stone

        Beautiful Black Madonna of France
        In El Barrio in my art studio
        Famous for the miracle of the fever stone
        As I meditated on my mat

        In El Barrio in my art studio
        You surrounded three-year-old me
        As I meditated on my mat
        I remembered my lost father

        You surrounded three-year-old me
        I love you as you are
        I remembered my lost father
        I missed him

Elaine Soto

I love you as you are

Le Puy en Veley

I missed him

I saw you

Rocamadour

We arrived at Rocamadour in the evening. Lorna made us wait until the following morning to see the Black Madonna. It is in a small Church started by St. Amador, a devotee of the Black Madonna. I love the mass I attended in this Church. The priest faced the congregation and spoke to us in English. He wanted to know who we were and what we were doing in France and at that Church. He was sincere, welcoming, and warm. He said mass and he gave us bread and wine instead of the host given in other Churches. It felt like a lovely meal with him, Christ, and the Black Madonna. The Black Madonna sat behind his shoulder on a high altar.

Our Lady of Rocamadour documents an old truth. It is that men and women are equal parts of an androgynous whole. It is each person's potential reality. Some Black Virgins like this one look masculine. Men need to relate to the power of the feminine within. If not, they become overwhelmed and possessed by it through their unconsciousness.

Giles Quispel, a Historian of Religion wrote that the Black Madonna symbolized earth. She is matter, the feminine in man, and the self in woman. Men and women need to become conscious of this primeval image of the Black Madonna. They need to integrate it within themselves. If they can, then they would be able to resolve the problems of materialism, racism, and women's liberation.

Rocamadour

15 MARY MAGDALENE

Sat in my studio at Taller Boricua

I felt very cold

Watercolor painting my handmade book

What I saw and learned about Mary Magdalene

I felt very cold

She was very close to the Master

What I saw and learned about Mary Magdalene

She was there at his feet on the cross

She was very close to the Master

She knew the All

She was there at his feet on the cross

The apostle who never denied him

She knew the All

Taught the other apostles

The apostle who never denied him

Mary Magdalene vilified and forced underground

Taught the other apostles

Watercolor painting my handmade book

Mary Magdalene vilified and forced underground

Sat in my studio at Taller Boricua

Santa Barbara
>
> Mary Magdalene underground
> A tower crowns your head
> Magdala means tower
> Sacred grail cup
>
> A tower crowns your head
> Santa Barbara
> Sacred grail cup
> Earth Goddess underground
>
> Santa Barbara
> Albigensian crusade
> Earth Goddess underground
> Believers massacred
>
> Albigensian crusade
> Apostle to the Apostles
> Believers massacred
> She knew the All
>
> Apostle to the Apostles
> Companion of Christ
> She knew the All
> The bride of Christ
>
> Companion of Christ
> Magdala means tower
> The bride of Christ
> Mary Magdalene underground

Elaine Soto

Santa Barbara

Margaret Starbird, a Roman Catholic scholar set out to refute the heresy. She did not believe in the marriage of Jesus and Mary Magdalene. Instead, she found evidence for the existence of the bride of Christ. She concluded that the Black Madonna may also be Mary Magdalene. According to her findings, Jesus as an Essene minister would have married at a young age. She wonders out loud if the story of the wedding feast at Cana is the story of their marriage. In it, Mary Magdalene anointed his head with spikenard. This was a ritual that a bride, performed to her betrothed in the wedding ceremony of that time. In France, some believe that Mary Magdalene is the Black Madonna. She is black because she represents something occult or hidden in the Church. The secret is the marriage of Jesus and Mary Magdalene. The image that follows is from one of my paintings "The Wedding". I found the image in a stained glass window in the Basilica at Montserrat Spain.

Elaine Soto

The Wedding

My Journey to the Black Madonna has taken me to the most maligned woman in Church history. It took me to Mary Magdalene. They called her a prostitute. They never said she was an Apostle. They never said Jesus married or that his wife was Mary Magdalene. I didn't know she wrote a gospel. I didn't learn that her gospel as well as the Gospels of Thomas and Phillip burned during the Council of Nicea in 321. They also burned documents connecting Jesus and Mary Magdalene as companions.

Her gospel is heretical according to the Church because she followed gnosis. Gnosis is knowledge/insight of the heart-intuitive thinking. It emphasizes creativity, perception, imagination, intuitive thinking, and encourages a free spirit. Students question, but they evolve and self-correct. They know themselves and the universal in all things. By studying the four elements: earth, water, air and fire one has direct experience. It takes you inward and you understand the All in All. According to Elaine Pagels, in Gnosticism, only one's own experience takes one closer to the truth. One can experience the divine without an intercessor. There are no punishments and an authority is not required. The experience has to be spontaneous and charismatic. The gospels of Mary Magdalene, Phillip, and Thomas threatened Church authorities. They accepted no creed, dogma, or canon. They took the power of original sin and atoning for it away from the Church. Rome tried to exterminate the Church of Mary Magdalene with the Crusades. They only drove it underground. They at the same time repressed the rights of women.

In the 11th and 12th Centuries, Gnosticism flourished. The troubadours converted the quest for the holy grail to the quest for women. Gnosticism influenced the artists of the Renaissance. The initiation aspect of the Black Virgin says everyone has to find his or her secret. Today the great search is for meaning. We seek it in relationships with the significant people in our lives. The Black Virgin is the feminine principle. She brings forth, nourishes, protects, heals, receives at death. She immortalizes her children who follow the way of nature. The light of nature tells us that life is a pilgrimage. In my search for the Black Madonna, I learned my secret was that I survived by repressing my feelings. They became unconscious. I survived, but I was not whole.

In 1945 archeologists found fourth-century papyrus manuscripts in Egypt. Monks hid them in caves after the Council of Nicea. In it were the Gospels of Phillip, Thomas, and Mary Magdalene. Greek, Coptic scholars translated the texts. They are the Nag Hammadi Library. In the texts, the voice of the Black Madonna explodes in "Thunder Perfect Mind". Conflicts among scholars limited access to the library for 50 years. The texts contradicted the dogma of different religions. They published the complete texts in English in 1977. But, in 2012 they discovered a new fragment of text. Karen L. King, a Harvard University professor, revealed the new fragment of the Gospel. In the text, Jesus refers to "my wife".

It took a few years to integrate the information that I discovered about the Black Madonna. It was easy to accept that she was a descendent of Isis and the ancient earth mother. She is Black after all. It was harder to integrate that the Madonna was black because she was also Mary Magdalene. It contradicted everything I learned in Catholic School. It made me hesitate to write this book. It made me hesitate as Mary Magdalene hesitated with Peter, the Apostle. She told Jesus that Peter made her hesitate to speak at their meetings because he hated the female race. At one of their meetings after she spoke, Peter said that Jesus should not listen to the words of a "mere woman". Although I am not a practicing Catholic, I do respect all religions. The training that I received as a Catholic also made me hesitate to speak up for fear of rejection.

Dr. Carl Gustav Jung studied Alchemy, a medieval form of the process of transformation. Fred Gustafson in his book on The Black Madonna draws on Jung's study of alchemy. He argues that devotion to the Black Madonna parallels the process of alchemy. Darkness or blackness is the initial stage of the alchemical work. This blackness in medieval times was the "raven". The blackness with which the alchemical process begins is also known as "nigredo". According to Jung, "to nourish the ravens is to nourish the contents of one's dark experiences". The possibility of wisdom comes from including the dark secrets of life. China Galland writes that "one is longing for darkness when one is longing for transformation". The darkness that brings greater balance, wholeness, integration, wisdom, and insight. The association of the word darkness with something evil is a cornerstone of racism.

"Racism is evil not darkness."

The Black Madonna is the compassionate one. She requires that we worship in spirit and in truth through the law written in our hearts. She requires that we follow the way of nature. The dark goddess is the magnetism of the universe-the Holy Spirit. "Life is a pilgrimage" a journey. The initiation aspect of the Black Madonna says everyone has to find his or her own dark secret.

In "Thunder, Perfect Mind" an ancient female deity describes herself as follows:

> "For I am the first and the last.
>
> I am the honored one and the scorned one.
>
> I am the whore and the holy one.
>
> I am the wife and the virgin.

I am the mother and the daughter."[2]

Lucia Chiavola Birnbaum argues that the Black Madonna is an amalgam of Christian, African, and Asian dark woman divinities. They combined them to convert people to Christianity. In her research, she discovered that areas of radical political activity in Italy are near sites of the Black Madonna. Equality, resistance to injustice, and regeneration are values associated with Black Madonnas. Marion Woodman, a Jungian Psychologist, disclosed that many of her patients reported dreams of the Black Madonna. She felt that the Black Madonna is erupting into consciousness. She is highlighting the racism and materialism that have overtaken our society.

---

[2] Robinson, James, N. The Nag Hamadi Library, p. 297.

Buoninsegna Madonna

16 HEALING

Met with Elena Avila
Collage of my father
I sat next to him talking
Wearing a frilly lavender dress

Collage of my father
His head leaning towards me
Wearing a frilly lavender dress
Gesturing with my hands

His head leaning towards me
They divorced after this photo
Gesturing with my hands
He did not keep his promise

They divorced after this photo
Mami did not accept his infidelity
He did not keep his promise
She left him

Mami did not accept his infidelity
I learned not to mention his name
She left him
I kept my love in a closed space

I learned not to mention his name
Mami said, "Your father doesn't care about you"
I kept my love in a closed space
"What do you want to say now?"

Mami said, "Your father doesn't care about you"
She said he left us
"What do you want to say now?"
"I love my father". I sobbed.

She said he left us

Elena placed me on a cot

"I love my father". I sobbed.

Three Curanderas dressed in white surrounded me

Elena placed me on a cot

Sprinkled me with agua florida

Three Curanderas dressed in white surrounded me

They passed fresh rosemary over my body

Sprinkled me with agua florida

Elena retrieved my three-year-old soul

They passed fresh rosemary sprigs over my body

The Curanderas prayed and consoled me

Elena retrieved my three-year-old soul

In a dream I saw her getting off a train…dirty and lost

The Curanderas prayed and consoled me

In another dream I saw her dressed in white…
dancing

In a dream I saw her getting off a train…dirty
and lost

Met with Elena Avila

In another dream I saw her dressed in white…
dancing

I sat next to him talking

My Journey to the Black Madonna

Papi

Pilgrimage

2018

I took a break from caretaking my mother who fell and broke her hip. She was wheelchair-bound and needed help with bathing, eating, and dressing. It was very painful to watch her as she became less able to do things on her own. She was always such a "mean go-getter". My husband and I visited her every day at the Senior Care house to make sure she was clean and fed. I wanted to make sure she wasn't neglected because she could be feisty. I loved helping her, but it was exhausting to care for her and work in my office. I was desperate for some rest and recuperation. I left my husband in charge of Mom, and I went on a Pilgrimage. It was a Colette tour to Fatima, Portugal, Lourdes, France, and Barcelona Spain. I added a side trip to Montserrat, my favorite Black Madonna site.

Fatima, Portugal

We arrived at the Fatima Hotel in Portugal by tour bus. I walked to the apparition site and photographed the Madonna. Our tour took us to the homes of the children who saw the Madonna. Lucia was 11 years old when the Madonna appeared to her and her two cousins. Francisco and Jacinta were 9 and 10 years old at the time of the apparition. The Madonna predicted that they would die young and they did. Lucia remained to recount the apparition. After our group tour, I explored the little shops nearby. At a gift shop, I met a lovely lady who sold rosaries and pictures of the Madonna. She told me she was a cousin of Jacinta, one of the children who saw the Madonna. I bought a beautiful print of Our Lady of Fatima from her.

I returned to the apparition site and prayed. Thinking about my mother leaving her body made me cry. There was a mass in the open-air chapel, but I didn't understand what the priest was saying and I left. After lunch, I went for a walk with two travel companions from Albuquerque. We visited some gift shops. I bought a conch shell-like those worn by the walkers on el Camino de Santiago de Compostela. I later gave the conch to my friend who later walked the Camino. The next morning, we traveled by Mercedes bus to Burgos Spain. We arrived at 6:30 pm and attended mass at the Cathedral with another Church group from Georgetown Texas. We had dinner at the Almirante hotel where we were staying. Our tour bus drove us to Burgos the next day. We visited the Gothic Cathedral in Burgos and the monastery of la Huelga. This monastery run by women. The abbess managed their assets. They were once very wealthy. But during the Napoleonic wars, the soldiers pillaged the coffins. They stole gold crowns and high-quality vestments. The nuns in the monastery gave communion. They also administered the sacraments until the 16th Century.

The next morning, we boarded the bus for Lourdes. It was a four-hour ride in the Pyrenees. They are the glue between the Iberian Peninsula where Portugal and Spain meet. I slept for most of the trip. I was getting a sore throat and I rested.

Visiting Fatima reminded me of when I saw the beautiful Madonna of Fatima in 1991 in a meditation. Fatima Madonna was one of my first Black Madonna paintings. When I saw images in my meditations, I painted them. I painted her the way that I saw her.

We were visiting Nan's mother, Angela in the Longwood section of the Bronx. She called us early that morning crying that someone stole her jewelry. Nan and I rushed over worried that she was in danger. When we arrived we found her pacing back and forth in a pink housedress and matching slippers in front of her door. "Gracias a Dios que llegaron." Thank God you got here.

"What happened?" Nan and I asked in unison.

"The neighbor's son stole my diamond earrings. I have looked everywhere and I can't find them. He got out of jail this week." She showed us an empty jewelry box. She lived in a one-bedroom apartment. Large and small cardboard boxes filled the living room, hallway, and bedroom. They contained material, thread, notions, and sewing supplies. Her industrial sewing machine sat in front of the windows in the living room. The windows lit up the living room and the adjacent dining area. She was an experienced seamstress who worked from home. She made wedding dresses and did alterations for people in the building and in her Church. I don't know how she could find anything in her apartment. There were boxes everywhere. It was overwhelming.

"I will change the lock," Nan said. He had brought tools and a spare lock from home. Nan was very handy and could repair almost anything if he took the time to study it. He even repaired his Chevy Chevette when it stalled on I-95 when we were on our way to a camping trip. He got out and checked under the hood. Something was loose in the engine and he didn't have the part. As he walked around the car, he noticed a metal washer on the floor. He tried fitting it where the car needed the part and the car turned on. I was very impressed! He was not only handsome with his dark curly hair and big eyes, but he was also creative.

It was Saturday morning and I needed a nap. I traveled to my office in Manhattan every day from Peekskill. It was three hours round trip. "I need a nap," I said.

"You can lay down on my bed," Angela said taking me into the bedroom. She moved a few boxes from the bed so I could lay down. There was a beautiful statue of Our Lady of Fatima on her antique dressing table. The Madonna wore a white gown and a white veil over her head. She held a rosary in her hand. Angela was the President of the Marian society in her Church. She and a small group of women carried the statue to the homes of the infirm and said the rosary for them. I admired the beauty of the Madonna's face as I laid down to rest and meditate.

While in meditation I felt a jolt and I saw the beautiful Lady of Fatima staring at me. The image lasted only a brief moment and disappeared. When I went to my studio I decided to paint her as Fatima Madonna. I made her door size in acrylic and oil pastels to refine her beautiful face. Her background is gold leaf.

Nan's mother called us at least three more times reporting a robbery. It coincided with not being able to find something. Nan and I returned and he changed the lock each time. The truth is she forgot where she put her things. Nan loved and humored her and changed the cylinder on her lock. When we moved to Colorado, she said she didn't want to stay in New York alone. We took her and over a hundred boxes with her belongings to Florissant. She moved next door with her older daughter and later she moved next door to us.

My Journey to the Black Madonna

Fatima Madonna

Lourdes, France

We arrived at our hotel in the late afternoon. I unpacked my bag and washed up. I took a walk to the cave where Our Lady appeared and a drop of water fell on my hand. There is a spring that runs out of the rock. We saw a movie on the bus that said the Madonna told her to dig up the earth with her hands and the water flowed. The Madonna appeared to her 19 times. Bernadette persisted in visiting the Madonna although the priests forbade it. We visited the home where she grew up. Her family owned a mill, but they sold it leaving them in dire circumstances.

Next, we went to mass in the crypt of the Church. I sang and prayed with the group but the air in the crypt made me cough and I left. I climbed up the steps to the old Church. It had beautiful stained glass windows and Milagros pinned on the wall near the altar. I sat and prayed for all my loved ones. I had intense pain in my left piriformis and I prayed for myself. Someone in our group suggested Voltadol Forte. I bought it in the pharmacy and applied it. The pain disappeared. Then I got a sore throat so I took a hot bath and went to bed early. The next day I went to the pharmacy and bought lidocaine throat lozenges. I developed swelling in my left ear. It felt like little demons were messing with me. Each time I went to the crypt for mass I started coughing so I left. I bought a large candle. I crossed the bridge to the other side of the Church and watched the outdoor mass given by cardinals at the grotto. It was quieter here and I prayed and took pictures. I shopped for a Madonna of Lourdes statue and some gifts at a shop near the hotel. I chatted with the store owner and I told her our next stop on the tour was Barcelona and Montserrat. We shared a love of Montserrat. After dinner, I went to the grotto for a Candlelight procession. I went with Rose and Patricia who were also on the tour. We lit each other's candles and marched saying the rosary in Spanish, English, French, and German. We visited the grotto and crossed the river to place our candles in the enclosures provided for them. We prayed for peace for our planet, took pictures of the grotto, and walked back to the hotel.

The next morning, we boarded the bus at 8 am for Barcelona. On the way, we stopped at Carcassonne, a medieval city for lunch. I later learned that this walled city was home to the Cathars. I wish we had stayed there a little longer to explore. Tours follow a tight schedule. I had lunch at a café. They served hot vervain tea, and rabbit stew. I ate the vegetables and left most of the rabbit in the stew. The meat was tough. I am a vegetarian and I don't usually eat meat. But, I wasn't feeling well and a hot soup hit the spot. On the bus, one of the ladies insisted on sitting next to me. I told her I preferred to sit alone because I wasn't feeling well. She was a very talkative lady and I didn't feel like talking. Reluctant to leave, she collected her belongings and moved to another seat. I slept and woke up at rest stops until we reached Barcelona.

The next morning, we visited La Sagrada Familia. The Cathedral created by Gaudi. This was my second visit here. It was still packed with people and rife with pickpockets. Our tour guide was on high alert here and took good care of us. No one got ripped off. The Cathedral was very developed since my visit 20 years before. Now we walked on the ground floor. Before it was all dirt, now it had tiles. Before we could only view the inside by climbing up a steep mountain of steps. It is amazing and worth risking the pickpockets. I took a lot of beautiful pictures of the church.

For the last day of the tour, I signed up for a short visit to Montserrat. A lot of people in the group joined me. As I walked around Montserrat and took pictures, an inner knowing told me that I needed to write. I love Montserrat. It is a sacred place.

When we returned from Montserrat, we dressed and went to an Italian restaurant at the seaport. There, we had a lovely farewell dinner of lobster, shrimp, scallops, and fresh fish. I enjoyed the pilgrimage but I missed Nan and Chula. I was happy to return home.

The Madonnas at Fatima and Lourdes are not Black, but they are powerful and also known for miracles. The Black Madonna of Montserrat is famous for its miracles. A lot of people continue to make pilgrimages to Montserrat as they do to Lourdes. My journey to the Black Madonna came out of a strong unconscious desire to become whole. I learned to transform old pain, grief, anger, and guilt. I turned those feelings into sources of love, harmony, and compassion.

Elaine Soto

Lourdes Cathedral

Pilgrims at Lourdes

Elaine Soto

Apparition Cave at Lourdes

My Journey to the Black Madonna

When the Black Madonna comes

    When the Black Madonna Comes
    This is the impulse of the good feminine
    The Psyche is growing
    In a spiritual direction

    This is the impulse of the good feminine
    Together with everyday life
    In a spiritual direction
    Together with the body, with the earth

    Together with everyday life
    This is the dawn of the feminine
    Together with the body, with the earth
    Women are realizing that man's way is not working

    This is the dawn of the feminine
    We must develop our capacities
    Women are realizing that man's way is not working
    We must follow our own inner guidance

    We must develop our capacities
    The Psyche is growing
    We must follow our own inner guidance
    When the Black Madonna comes

Photo credit: Donald Monceda

About the Author

Elaine Soto is an artist, psychologist. She received a Ford Foundation Doctoral Fellowship in 1972. She attended the Harvard Graduate School of Education and New York University. She received a Master's and a Ph.D. in Education and Psychology. She studied art nondegree at the School of Visual Arts. In 1986 Taller Boricua invited her to be an artist in residence. She remained there for 15 years. As an artist in residence, she researched and painted the Black Madonna. With the Taller, she created expressive art workshops for the community. At Union Theological Seminary, she taught art and community development. "Dancing in the Flames", a movie about Marion Woodman features her paintings. Her work is also in the book Dark Mother, by Lucia Chiavola Birnbaum. She lives and works in Albuquerque, New Mexico.

Her artwork is on view at:
        https://www.elainesoto.com

BIBLIOGRAPHY

Albareda, Anselmo, M. <u>Historia De Montserrat</u>, De L'Abadia De Montserrat, Spain, 1974.

Belloni, Alessandra. <u>Healing Journeys with the Black Madonna</u>, Bear & Company, Rochester, Vermont, 2019.

Begg, Ean. <u>The Cult of the Black Virgin</u>, Penguin Books, New York, 1985.

Bernal, Martin. <u>Black Athena</u>, Rutgers University Press, New Jersey, 1991.

Birnbaum Chiavola, Lucia. <u>Dark Mother</u>, Authors Choice Press, Lincoln, NE, 2001.

Birnbaum Chiavola, Lucia. <u>Black Madonnas, feminism, religion & politics in Italy</u>. Northeastern University Press, Boston, Mass., 1993.

Davies, Stevan. <u>The Gospel of Thomas</u>, Skylight Paths, Vermont, 2002.

Facaros, Dana & Pauls, Michael. <u>Spain</u>, Globe Pequot Press, Conn., 1992.

Foundation for Inner Peace. <u>A Course in Miracles</u>, Coleman Graphics, NY 1975

Gadon, Elinor, W. <u>The Once and Future Goddess</u>, Harper-Collins, New York, 1989.

Galland, China. <u>Longing for Darkness</u>, Penguin, New York, 1990.

Gardner, Laurence. Bloodline of the Holy Grail, Element Books Limited, Great Britain, 1996.

Getty, Adele. Goddess, Mother of Living Nature, Thames & Hudson, Ltd., London, 1990.

Gustafson, Fred. The Black Madonna, Sigo Press, Mass., 1990.

King, Karen L. The Gospel of Mary of Magdala, Polebridge, Press, Santa Rosa, CA, 2003.

King, Karen L. "Harvard Theological Review", The Gospel of Jesus's Wife. April 2014, Vol.107/Issue 02, pp. 131-159.

Le Loup, Jean Yves. The Gospel of Mary Magdalene, Inner Traditions, Vermont, 2002.

Méndez de Guzmán, Noelle. La Verdadera Historia de la Aparición de la Virgen Del Rosario, True Way Productions, Inc., Mary's House Division, México, 1989,1990.

Meyer, Marvin & De Boer, Esther A. The Gospels of Mary : The Secret Tradition of Mary Magdalene the Companion of Jesus, Harper Collins, New York, 2004.

Napier, Jeff, 291 Maya Angelou Quotes, 2014.

Pagels, Elaine. The Gnostic Gospels, Vintage Books, New York, 1989.

Perera Brinton, Sylvia. Descent to the Goddess. A Way of Initiation for Women. Inner City Books, Toronto Canada, 1981.

Robinson, James, M. The Nag Hammadi Library, Harper One, New York, 1988.

Rufus, Arneli, S. & Lawson, Kristan. Goddess Sites : Europe, Harper Collins, New York, 1991.

Van Sertima, Ivan, Editor. Black Women in Antiquity, Transaction Publishers, New Brunswick & London, 1988.

Vidal, Teodoro. Los Milagros en cera y en metal de Puerto Rico, USA, 1974.

Walker, Barbara, G. The Women's Encyclopedia of Myths & Secrets, Harper & Row, New York, 1983.

Woodman, Marion & Dickson, Elinor. Dancing in the Flames, The Dark Goddess in the Transformation of Consciousness, Shambhala, Boston, 1997.

Made in United States
Orlando, FL
25 November 2022

25012125R00107